INS 22

Personal Insurance

Review Notes

About This Study Aid

This guide was developed to help you study the course material and prepare for the examination. Each assignment is outlined according to the Educational Objectives (EOs). As a study aid, this material is not intended to present all of the information found in the textbook(s), course guide, or online modules published by The Institutes. Instead, we strongly encourage you to use this study aid to supplement the course materials.

Some EOs involve the application of skills in a case study or situation. The material presented provides information to help you acquire the skill, but cases or scenario situations are not provided within this material. You may find such cases and scenarios within the textbook(s), course guide, or online modules.

1st Edition • 1st Printing • December 2010

ISBN: 978-0-89463-426-0

Dependent people need others to get what they want. Independent people can get what they want through their own efforts. **Interdependent** *people combine their own efforts with the efforts of others to achieve their greatest success.*

—Stephen Covey

The Institutes™

Proven Knowledge. Powerful Results.

Think
s.m.a.r.t.

...and Achieve
Your Greatest
Success.

Time Savers

We know your life is busy, and that's why we've developed some tips to help you make the most of your study time. By following these tips, you'll study more effectively—and couldn't we all use a little more free time?

To be time-efficient, we recommend that you:

Order your copy of *How to Prepare for Institutes Exams* or download it free from our Web site. This booklet will give you helpful study and exam-taking tips.

Create a plan for study time. A study schedule will help you identify up front the time you will need to study the course and the dates when you plan to study. Simply use the worksheet that follows to enter this information and, when you're finished, block out those dates on your calendar. This is an investment in yourself!

Start studying right away. If you wait to start studying, you create a time crunch near exam time. Getting a strong start on your studying keeps you on track for the exam date and may allow you a week or two to review all the assignments together.

Decide how you learn best. The Institutes offer a variety of study materials to help you learn in the way that you feel most comfortable. Read the textbook or complete the modules for the full course content. Practice what you're learning with the course guide or Knowledge Check questions. Use the flash cards to remember Key Words and Phrases. Or, use the SMART Online Practice Exam product, if available for this course, to test your knowledge. Use the best combination of study tools for your learning style to help you retain your new knowledge.

Consider joining a class. Some people learn best with the structure and interaction of a formal class. We offer both online classes and public classes. The online classes combine the flexibility of self-study with the support of a knowledgeable instructor. Public classes are in-person classes offered by third-party vendors in your area. If structure helps you maximize your use of time, choose a class today. See our Web site for more information about either of these class options.

Call us if you need assistance. We believe in helping you achieve powerful results. This means supplying prompt answers to your questions, online counseling, and telephone and e-mail Customer Service. Call us with any questions at (800) 644-2101, or send an email to customerservice@TheInstitutes.org.

Good luck with your course!

Study Timetable

To help you make the best use of your time, keep the following suggestions in mind as you create your study timetable:

- Allocate study time conservatively; give yourself ample time to digest the material.
- Limit your study time to two hours or less on a given day.
- Vary the types of study tools you use, for maximum retention.
- Study when you have unexpected free time.
- Keep to your study timetable to avoid last-minute "cramming."
- Enter this study timetable into your daily calendar.
- Evaluate your timetable periodically, and make adjustments as necessary.

The Sample Study Timetable below shows what one student's study plan might look like using the textbook and course guide. A student taking online courses will be able to allocate study time based on the length of each module. Take 15 minutes to fill out your own Study Timetable. Doing this will ensure that you have carefully considered the dates and amounts of time you will need for each assignment. Make the most of your study time by making it efficient!

Assignment # and Title (From Course Guide)	Assignment Notes	Study Time	Study Dates	Activities	Assignment End Date
Assignment 1, Risk	Important foundation concepts. Will read carefully.	45 min. / 45 min. / 30 min.	5/9 / 5/10 / 5/11	Read Text / Complete Course Guide / Online Practice Exam	5/12
Assignment 2, Ethics	I am familiar with some of this content from prior ethics training.	30 min. / 1 hour	5/15 / 5/17	Read Review Notes / Complete Course Guide	5/19
Assignment 3, Managing Risk	A number of key words in this assignment	1 hour / 1 hour	5/23 / 5/24	Read Text / Practice Flash Cards	5/26
Assignment 15, Allocating Costs		1 hour	8/15		8/17

Exam Date: Sept. 9, 2011

Study Timetable

Exam Date: _____

Assignment # and Title (From Course Guide)	Assignment Notes	Study Time	Study Dates	Activities	Assignment End Date

Personal Insurance Overview

Educational Objective 1
Summarize the three elements of loss exposures.

Key Points:

Conditions or situations that expose assets to loss are called loss exposures. Every loss exposure has three elements: asset exposed to loss, cause of loss, and financial consequences of loss.

A. An asset exposed to loss can be any item with value that is exposed to a possible reduction in that value due to loss.

B. A cause of loss (or peril) is the means by which an asset can be reduced in value. Individuals and families should, to the extent possible, identify and guard against causes of loss that could present the possibility of damage to or a reduction in value of their assets.

C. An asset exposed to loss is affected by a cause of loss, generating a financial consequence. The financial consequences of a loss depend on the type of asset exposed to loss, the cause of loss, and the severity of the loss.

Study Tips

The application questions will help you apply what you've learned. Take some time to complete those questions and practice what you've learned.

Educational Objective 2

Describe the property loss exposures that individuals and families might face in terms of each of the following:

- **The assets exposed to loss**

- **The causes of loss**

- **The financial consequences of loss**

Key Points:

A property loss exposure is any condition or situation that presents the possibility of a property loss. Property loss exposures can be examined in terms of three loss exposure elements: assets exposed to loss, causes of loss, and financial consequences of loss.

A. Assets exposed to loss are any items of property that have value. Property includes real property and personal property.

    1. Real property consists of land, buildings, other structures attached to the land, whatever is growing on the land, and anything embedded in the land. All real property is tangible property having a physical form that can be seen or touched.

    2. Personal property is all property other than real property.

        a. A general sampling of some personal property loss exposures includes those experienced by homeowners, renters, or condominium owners, who likely own furniture, as well as televisions and other electronic entertainment equipment.

        b. Personal property can include intangible property such as patents or copyrights (which are also often referred to as intellectual property).

B. Many causes of loss (or perils) can damage or destroy both real and personal property.

    1. In terms of real property, causes of loss faced by individuals and families include fire damage to a dwelling or storage shed, lightning damage to a tree, earthquake damage to a swimming pool, and wind damage to roof shingles.

    2. Personal property causes of loss can include theft of a car or damage to a car in an accident, disappearance of luggage and its contents while the owner is on vacation, and loss of a diamond that falls from its setting in a ring. Even damage to a motorboat that collides with a dock is a personal property loss.

C. Financial consequences of loss—When property is damaged or destroyed, individuals and families sustain certain financial consequences, which can include one or more of the following:

1. Reduction in value of property—the difference between the value of the property before the loss (pre-loss value) and after the loss (post-loss value)

2. Increased expenses—expenses in addition to normal living expenses that are necessary because of the loss

3. Lost income—loss of income that results if property is damaged

Educational Objective 3

Describe the liability loss exposures that individuals and families might face in terms of each of the following:

- **The assets exposed to loss**

- **The causes of loss**

- **The financial consequences of loss**

Key Points:

All individuals and families, through owning property, driving a car, or entering into contracts with others, face a potential reduction in their assets from the possibility of being sued or being held responsible for someone else's injury.

A. Assets Exposed to Loss

These are money or other financial assets.

1. A liability loss can result from property ownership or from the actions of individuals or family members.

2. Damages awarded in a liability judgment take the following forms:

   a. General damages

   b. Special damages

   c. Punitive or exemplary damages

B. Causes of Loss

These are the claim of liability or the filing of a lawsuit. Civil law involves the settlement of disputes between individuals and the indemnification for wrongs committed against individuals and provides the legal foundation of insurance.

1. Tort liability—Arises from acts of negligence, intentional torts, or absolute liability.

2. Contractual liability—Arises when an individual enters into a contract or an agreement.

3. Statutory liability—Exists because of the passage of a statute or law.

C. Financial Consequences of Loss

When a liability claim occurs, an individual or a family can suffer the following two major financial consequences:

1. Costs of investigation and defense

2. Money damages awarded if the defense is not successful or if the claim is settled out of court

    a. In theory, financial consequences of a liability loss exposure are limitless.

    b. Claims settled before they reach court are negotiated and are therefore generally less expensive.

    c. Some jurisdictions limit the amount that can be taken in a claim, however liability claims can result in loss of most or all of a person's assets as well as in a claim on future income.

Educational Objective 4

Describe the personal financial planning loss exposures that individuals and families might face in terms of each of the following:

- **The assets exposed to loss**
- **The causes of loss**
- **The financial consequences of loss**

Key Points:

Certain personal financial planning loss exposures can cause significant financial difficulty for individuals and families.

A. The three elements of personal financial planning loss exposures are as follows:

  1. Assets exposed to loss

  2. Causes of loss

  3. Financial consequences of loss

B. Personal financial planning loss exposures that can cause significant financial difficulty for individuals and families include the following:

  1. Retirement loss exposures

  a. Assets exposed to loss include regular employment income and the related benefits, such as health insurance.

  b. The immediate cause of loss usually is voluntary retirement; actual retirement-related loss stems from failure to maintain resources sufficient to sustain a desired lifestyle or from an underestimation of the length of the retirement period.

  c. If replacement income from Social Security benefits, private retirement plans, and personal savings is inadequate, the retired worker's standard of living may be reduced significantly. If the retired worker lives unusually long, incurs catastrophic medical expenses, or requires long-term care in a nursing facility, the financial consequences of retirement may result in insufficient income to sustain the worker and his or her family.

  2. Premature death loss exposures

  a. The assets exposed to loss include the expected income on which his or her family or heirs rely.

  b. Causes of loss associated with premature death include accident, illness, or the intentional taking of life.

    c. If replacement income from life insurance, financial assets, or existing income from other sources does not meet the deceased individual's family's needs, it is likely to experience considerable financial hardship.

3. Health and disability loss exposures
   a. The assets exposed to loss include income if the person is unable to work, as well any individual or family savings and other financial assets, which may be depleted by health-related expenditures.
   b. The causes of loss associated with health and disability loss exposures are chronic illness or physical or mental disability.
   c. An individual may incur catastrophic medical expenses as a result of poor health or disability. Lacking health insurance or savings to pay such expenses, a sick or injured person will be exposed to financial insecurity, which may be compounded by reduction or elimination of income if the person is unable to work.

4. Unemployment loss exposures
   a. The assets exposed to loss by unemployment include income and employer-provided benefits.
   b. The causes of loss in cases of unemployment may be voluntary or involuntary.
   c. The financial consequences are loss of earnings and other employer-provided benefits, such as health insurance and monetary contributions toward retirement.

Educational Objective 5

Demonstrate how the six steps of the risk management process can guide individuals and families in their risk management decisions.

Key Points:

A. Step 1: Identifying Loss Exposures

   1. Friends and family members can help identify loss exposures by sharing their own loss histories and experience.

   2. The insurance agent may provide checklists that focus on common sources of loss exposures and use his or her own experience and training to help individuals and families determine areas that they may need to address with risk management techniques.

B. Step 2: Analyzing Loss Exposures

   1. This analysis entails estimating the likely significance of possible losses identified in step one. Together, these two steps constitute the process of assessing loss exposures, and they are therefore often considered the most important components of the risk management process.

   2. When organizations analyze the loss exposures they have identified, they focus on the following four dimensions:

      a. Loss frequency—the number of losses within a specific time period

      b. Loss severity—the amount, in dollars, of a loss for a specific occurrence

      c. Total dollar losses—the total dollar amount of losses for all occurrences during a specific period

      d. Timing—when losses occur and when loss payments are made

C. Step 3: Examining the Feasibility of Risk Management Techniques

   1. Loss exposures can be addressed through risk control techniques and risk financing techniques. Unless they are entirely avoiding a loss exposure, individuals should typically apply at least one risk control technique and one risk financing technique to each of their significant loss exposures.

   2. Individuals and families should examine all available risk control and risk financing techniques and determine which are feasible for them.

D. Step 4: Selecting the Appropriate Risk Management Techniques—Selecting the most appropriate combination of risk management techniques is usually based on quantitative financial considerations as well as qualitative, nonfinancial considerations.

    1. Most households choose risk management techniques by using financial criteria. Households must compare the potential costs of completely untreated loss exposures with the costs of possible risk management techniques when considering whether a technique is economical.

    2. A household's nonfinancial goals can constrain its financial goals, leading to the selection of risk management techniques that, although best for that family, might be inconsistent with its value maximization goal.

E. Step 5: Implementing the Selected Risk Management Techniques—Implementing risk management techniques may involve any of the following measures:

    1. Purchasing loss reduction devices

    2. Contracting for loss prevention services

    3. Funding retention programs

    4. Implementing and continually reinforcing loss control programs

    5. Selecting agents or brokers, insurers, and other insurance providers who can suggest ways to deal with specific loss exposures

    6. Requesting insurance policies and paying premiums for loss exposures that an individual does not want to retain (or is required to have by statute or by a lender)

    7. Creating and updating a list of possessions that may be subject to loss

F. Step 6: Monitoring Results and Revising the Risk Management Program

    1. Individuals and families must monitor and periodically review their risk management program to ensure that it is achieving expected results.

    2. They also should adjust it to accommodate changes in loss exposures and in the availability or cost-effectiveness of alternative risk management techniques.

    3. Additionally, if individuals engage in new hobbies with significant loss exposures (such as coin collecting or the acquisition of expensive art), they should adopt additional risk management techniques to deal with these exposures.

Educational Objective 6

Describe how risk control and risk financing techniques are used by individuals and families.

Key Points:

Individuals and families may use risk control or risk financing techniques to manage risks and ensure their well-being, financial stability, and security.

A. Risk control techniques aim to reduce either loss frequency or loss severity, or to make losses more predictable. These techniques fall into one of the following six broad categories:

1. Avoidance—The goal of avoidance is not simply to reduce loss frequency, but to eliminate any possibility of loss. In some cases, avoidance is at least impractical, if not impossible.

2. Loss prevention—This technique is implemented to break the sequence of events that leads to the loss.

    a. Determining effective loss prevention measures usually requires carefully studying how particular losses are caused.

    b. A loss prevention measure may reduce the frequency of losses from one loss exposure but increase the frequency or severity of losses from other loss exposures.

3. Loss reduction—Some loss reduction measures can prevent losses as well as reduce them.

4. Separation—The intent of separation is to reduce the severity of an individual loss at a single location. However, by creating multiple locations, separation may increase loss frequency.

5. Duplication—Examples of duplication include maintaining a second set of records; spare parts for autos, household appliances, or yard machinery; and copies of keys.

6. Diversification—By spreading risk, diversification reduces loss severity and can make losses more predictable.

▶▶

B. Risk financing techniques can help individuals and families recover from loss or damage that might otherwise cause them significant financial impairment. Traditionally, risk financing measures generally have been categorized as either retention techniques or transfer techniques.

1. Retention

   a. Usually, a family deliberately uses retention only to treat loss exposures that are within its financial means. However, retention is the default risk financing technique if a risk is not identified or transferred.

   b. Most families and individuals do not retain losses on a pre-planned, structured basis. They generally pay for retained losses with reserve savings or may change budgeting priorities to pay for them.

   c. Retention can be planned or unplanned; complete or partial; or funded or unfunded.

2. Transfer

   a. Insurance is the most prevalent form of risk transfer.

   - The insurance buyer substitutes a small, certain financial cost, the insurance premium, for the possibility of a large, uncertain financial loss, which is paid by the insurer.

   - Although insurance is only one approach to risk transfer, it is frequently the only method of risk transfer available to individuals and families.

   b. Some risk transfer techniques, such as a hold-harmless agreement, do not involve insurance. A hold-harmless agreement may be included in an apartment lease, for instance.

   c. Hedging is a noninsurance risk transfer technique in which one asset (money) is paid to offset the risk associated with another asset.

Educational Objective 7
Explain how personal insurance is used as a risk management technique.

Key Points:

Personal insurance consists of three layers: social programs of insurance, group insurance, and individual insurance. The most widely purchased kinds of insurance from these three layers address the following loss exposures:

A. Property and Liability Loss Exposures
  1. Property loss exposures stem from a legal interest in both real property and personal property.
  2. Liability loss exposures originate from the possibility of being sued or being held responsible for someone else's injury.
  3. Auto insurance covers auto-related property and liability loss exposures.
  4. Homeowners insurance protects against real and personal property loss exposures as well as liability loss exposures.
  5. For liability protection beyond that offered by homeowners and auto policies, individuals and families can purchase umbrella liability protection.
  6. Insurers require the insured to retain a predetermined portion of the cost of a covered loss in the form of a deductible.

B. Retirement Loss Exposures
  1. The assets exposed to loss when an individual retires are regular employment income and the related benefits of employment, such as health insurance.
  2. Many individuals and families maintain savings plans and pension plans to help them prepare for retirement. Some may choose through an insurance mechanism to convert their savings to annuities, which guarantee a monthly payment for life.
  3. Families and individuals also can mitigate the financial uncertainty associated with retirement loss exposures by participating in individual retirement accounts (IRAs) and 401(k) savings plans.
  4. The federal government's Social Security program provides financial benefits to retirees and their families.
  5. Many workers who opt to work beyond their full retirement also participate in employer-sponsored group pension plans, defined benefit plans, and defined contribution plans.

C. Premature Death Loss Exposures

1. The assets exposed to loss as the result of an individual's premature death include the expected income on which his or her family or heirs rely.

2. One of the most effective ways for families to manage the premature death loss exposure is to purchase a life insurance policy. The amount of life insurance that an individual or family should purchase can be determined by the needs-based approach or the human life value approach.

D. Health and Disability Loss Exposures

1. Many employers contribute a portion of the premiums for their employees' health and disability insurance.

2. Individual and group health and disability insurance may be more important to an individual or family than life insurance.

3. Three prominent government programs (social insurance programs) that also provide health and disability benefits are Medicare, Medicaid, and workers compensation.

4. Individuals and families also may consider purchasing long-term health care insurance to help mitigate the potentially high costs of extended medical care or custodial care they may require later in life in a nursing home, hospital, or in their home.

E. Unemployment Loss Exposures

1. The assets exposed to loss by unemployment include income and employer-provided benefits.

2. All state governments sponsor unemployment compensation programs that pay benefits to covered individuals who are involuntarily unemployed.

Educational Objective 8

Summarize the contents of the six common categories of policy provisions of a property-casualty insurance policy.

Key Points:

A. Declarations—Contains the standard information that has been "declared" by both the insured and the insurer and information unique to the particular policy.

  1. The declarations typically appear as the first page in the policy and contain the following information:

    a. Policy or policy number

    b. Policy inception and expiration dates (policy period)

    c. Name of the insurer

    d. Name of the insurance agent

    e. Name of the insured(s)

    f. Names of persons or organizations whose additional interests are covered

    g. Mailing address of the insured

    h. Physical address and description of the covered property or operations

    i. Numbers and edition dates of all attached forms and endorsements

    j. Dollar amounts of applicable policy limits

    k. Dollar amounts of applicable deductibles

    l. Premium

  2. In some cases, other policy forms or endorsements contain information that qualifies as part of the declarations, often referred to as a "schedule."

B. Definitions—Defines the terms used throughout the entire policy or form. Undefined words and phrases are interpreted according to the following rules of policy interpretation:

  1. Everyday words are given their ordinary meanings.

  2. Technical words are given their technical meanings.

  3. Words with an established legal meaning are given their legal meanings.

  4. Consideration is also given to the local, cultural, and trade-usage meanings of words, if applicable.

C. Insuring Agreements—States the promise of coverage the insurer makes to the insured. Policies typically contain an insuring agreement for each coverage they provide.

D. Conditions—Contains the insurer's and the insured's contractual duties for enforcement of the policy's insuring agreement.

E. Exclusions—Limit and clarify coverages granted by the insurer. Specifying what the insurer does not intend to cover is a way of clarifying what the insurer does intend to cover. The six purposes of exclusions are as follows:

1. Eliminate coverage for uninsurable loss exposures.
2. Assist in managing moral and morale hazards.
3. Reduce likelihood of coverage duplications.
4. Eliminate coverages not needed by the typical insured.
5. Eliminate coverages requiring special treatment.
6. Assist in keeping premiums reasonable.

F. Miscellaneous Provisions—Specify the relationship between the insured and the insurer or help establish working procedures for implementing the policy.

1. Even if the insured does not follow the procedures specified in the miscellaneous provisions, the insurer may still be required to fulfill its contractual promises.
2. Miscellaneous provisions often are unique to particular types of insurers.

Educational Objective 9
Describe the primary methods of insurance policy analysis.

Key Points:

A. Pre-Loss Policy Analysis—Relies on scenario analysis to determine the extent of coverage (if any) the policy provides for the losses generated by a given scenario.

   1. For insureds, the primary source of information used is their past loss experience. Another source of information is the insurance producer or customer service representative consulted in the insurance transaction.

   2. One of the limitations of scenario analysis is that, because the number of possible loss scenarios is theoretically infinite, it is impossible to account for every possibility.

B. Post-Loss Policy Analysis—When an insured reports a loss, the insurer must determine whether the loss triggers coverage and, if so, its extent.

   1. The DICE (an acronym representing the policy provision categories: declarations, insuring agreements, conditions, and exclusions) method is a systematic review of all the categories of property-casualty policy provisions. The following four steps are used to determine whether a policy provides coverage:

      a. Step 1—An examination of the declarations page determines whether the information provided by the insured precludes coverage. If nothing in the declarations precludes coverage, the insurance professional would proceed to step 2.

      b. Step 2—An analysis of the insuring agreement determines whether a provision in an insuring agreement precludes coverage. If coverage is precluded, the claim will be denied. If nothing in the insuring agreement precludes coverage, the insurance professional proceeds to step 3.

      c. Step 3—Analyzing conditions can help the insurance professional clarify important points, such as whether any of the following are true:

         • Fulfillment of certain conditions is required for there to be an enforceable policy.

         • Coverage will be denied if an insured party breaches a policy condition.

- Coverage triggers and coverage territory restrictions affect the loss.
- Conditions concerning the rights and duties of both parties to maintain the insurance policy apply.
- Post-loss duties of the insured and the insurer affect coverage.
- Conditions have been or need to be adhered to regarding claim disputes.
- Subrogation and salvage rights and conditions must be considered.

   d. Step 4—An analysis of policy exclusions and any other policy provisions not already analyzed, including endorsements and miscellaneous provisions, determines whether they would preclude coverage.

2. After using the DICE method to ascertain whether the claim is covered, the insurer must then determine how much is payable under the policy.

Key Words and Phrases:

Key Words

Loss exposure
Any condition or situation that presents a possibility of loss, whether or not an actual loss occurs.

Cause of loss (peril)
The actual means by which property is damaged or destroyed.

Property loss exposure
A condition that presents the possibility that a person or an organization will sustain a loss resulting from damage (including destruction, taking, or loss of use) to property in which that person or organization has a financial interest.

Real property (realty)
Tangible property consisting of land, all structures permanently attached to the land, and whatever is growing on the land.

Personal property
All tangible or intangible property that is not real property.

Liability loss exposure
Any condition or situation that presents the possibility of a claim alleging legal responsibility of a person or business for injury or damage suffered by another party.

Damages
Money claimed by, or a monetary award to, a party who has suffered bodily injury or property damage for which another party is legally responsible.

General damages
A monetary award to compensate a victim for losses, such as pain and suffering, that do not involve specific measurable expenses.

Special damages
A form of compensatory damages that awards a sum of money for specific, identifiable expenses associated with the injured person's loss, such as medical expenses or lost wages.

Punitive damages (exemplary damages)
A payment awarded by a court to punish a defendant for a reckless, malicious, or deceitful act to deter similar conduct; the award need not bear any relation to a party's actual damages.

Civil law
A classification of law that applies to legal matters not governed by criminal law and that protects rights and provides remedies for breaches of duties owed to others.

Tort
A wrongful act or an omission, other than a crime or a breach of contract, that invades a legally protected right.

Negligence
The failure to exercise the degree of care that a reasonable person in a similar situation would exercise to avoid harming others.

Personal financial planning loss exposures
Life, health and retirement related loss exposures.

Temporary partial disability (TPD)
A disability caused by a work-related injury or disease that temporarily limits the extent to which a worker can perform job duties; the worker is eventually able to return to full duties and hours.

Temporary total disability (TTD)
A disability caused by a work-related injury or disease that temporarily renders an injured worker unable to perform any job duties for a period of time; the worker eventually makes a full recovery and can resume all job duties.

Permanent partial disability in workers compensation
A disability caused by a work-related injury or disease that impairs the injured employee's earning capacity for life, but the employee is able to work at reduced efficiency.

Permanent total disability in workers compensation
A disability caused by a work-related injury or disease that renders an injured employee unable to ever return to gainful employment.

Risk management process
The method of making, implementing, and monitoring decisions that minimize the adverse effects of risk on an organization.

Risk control
A conscious act or decision not to act that reduces the frequency and/or severity of losses or makes losses more predictable.

Risk financing
A conscious act or decision not to act that generates the funds to pay for losses and risk control measures or to offset variability in cash flows.

Avoidance
A risk control technique that involves ceasing or never undertaking an activity so that the possibility of a future loss occurring from that activity is eliminated.

Loss prevention
A risk control technique that reduces the frequency of a particular loss.

Loss reduction
A risk control technique that reduces the severity of a particular loss.

Separation
A risk control technique that isolates loss exposures from one another to minimize the adverse effect of a single loss.

Duplication
A risk control technique that uses backups, spares, or copies of critical property, information, or capabilities and keeps them in reserve.

Diversification
A risk control technique that spreads loss exposures over numerous projects, products, markets, or regions.

Retention
A risk financing technique by which losses are retained by generating funds within the organization to pay for the losses.

Insurance
A risk management technique that transfers the potential financial consequences of certain specified loss exposures from the insured to the insurer.

Transfer
In the context of risk management, a risk financing technique by which the financial responsibility for losses and variability in cash flows is shifted to another party.

Workers compensation
A system that pays lost wages, medical and vocational rehabilitation expenses, and death benefits to injured workers or their dependents for employment-related injuries and diseases.

Policy provisions
Any phrase or clause in an insurance policy that describes the policy's coverages, exclusions, limits, conditions, or other features.

Declarations page (declarations, or dec.)
An insurance policy information page or pages providing specific details about the insured and the subject of the insurance.

Endorsement
A document that amends an insurance policy.

Definitions
A preliminary section of a homeowners policy identifying the insured, the insurance company, and the commonly used terms found through-out the policy.

Insuring agreement
A statement in an insurance policy that the insurer will, under described circumstances, make a loss payment or provide a service.

Policy condition
Any provision that qualifies an otherwise enforceable promise made in the policy.

Exclusion
A policy provision that eliminates coverage for specified exposures.

Automobile Insurance and Society

2

Educational Objective 1

Evaluate each of the following approaches to compensating automobile accident victims:

- **Tort liability system**

- **Financial responsibility laws**

- **Compulsory insurance laws**

- **Uninsured motorists coverage**

- **Underinsured motorists coverage**

- **No-fault insurance**

Key Points:

A. The tort liability system is based on fault.

   1. Most tort liability cases arise out of negligence.

      a. Injured auto accident victims must prove that another party was at fault before they can collect damages from that party.

      b. The amount of damages can be determined through negotiations between the two parties or through a lawsuit and court settlement.

   2. Advantages

      a. The tort liability system provides a remedy for victims of negligent or irresponsible drivers who cause accidents.

      b. Injured victims are compensated for their costs, and the costs are allocated to the responsible party.

      c. The system may act as an incentive for drivers to act responsibly in order to avoid lawsuits.

   3. Disadvantages

      a. Substantial delays in reaching a settlement either through negotiation or through the courts

      b. Significant legal and administrative costs related to settling lawsuits or pursuing a case to judgment

      c. Punitive damage awards by juries that may be considered excessive

Study Tips

Many of the exam questions are based on the Key Words and Phrases—remember to review them thoroughly.

B. Financial responsibility laws require motorists to provide proof of financial responsibility (such as liability insurance) under certain circumstances. Failure to provide the required proof can result suspension of the motorist's driver's license and vehicle registration.

  1. Proof of financial responsibility is required in the following circumstances:

    a. After an auto accident involving bodily injury or property damage exceeding a certain dollar amount

    b. After a conviction for certain serious offenses, such as drunk driving or reckless driving, or after losing a driver's license because of repeated violations

    c. Upon failure to pay a final judgment that results from an auto accident

  2. Advantages

    a. These laws provide some protection to victims of auto accidents against irresponsible drivers.

    b. They work in conjunction with the tort liability system to ensure that at-fault drivers will not only be held liable for accidents they cause but also have a mechanism in place to pay for the financial consequences of those accidents.

  3. Disadvantages

    a. Most financial responsibility requirements become effective only after an accident, a conviction, or a judgment.

    b. Persons injured by uninsured drivers, hit-and-run drivers, or drivers of stolen cars might not be compensated.

    c. Most financial responsibility laws set minimum financial requirements, which may not fully compensate a victim.

C. Most states have compulsory auto insurance laws that require auto liability insurance for all motorists to drive legally within the state.

  1. In lieu of auto insurance, a motorist can post a bond or deposit cash or securities to guarantee financial responsibility in the event of an auto accident.

  2. Many states require the insurer to verify insurance coverage and/or to notify the state if a policy is cancelled or is not renewed.

  3. Other states require insurers to submit information regarding the automobile insurance policies they have issued within that jurisdiction.

  4. Advantages

    a. Motorists must provide proof of financial responsibility before an accident occurs.

▶▶

    b. Compulsory insurance laws work in conjunction with the tort liability system to ensure compensation for victims of auto accidents that are the fault of other drivers.

  5. Disadvantages

    a. Compulsory insurance laws do not guarantee compensation to all accident victims.

    b. The required minimum amount of insurance may not meet the full needs of accident victims.

    c. Some drivers do not insure their vehicles because insurance is too costly. Others let coverage lapse after demonstrating proof of insurance to satisfy vehicle registration requirements.

    d. Insurers argue that compulsory laws restrict their freedom to select profitable insureds. In addition, insurers fear that state regulators might deny needed rate increases, resulting in underwriting losses.

    e. Consumer advocates argue that if insurers are allowed to increase rates to compensate for accepting all applicants for insurance, rates might become unfairly high for good drivers.

    f. Compulsory insurance laws do not prevent or reduce the number of automobile accidents.

  6. Several states have implemented measures intended to respond to the disadvantages of compulsory insurance.

    a. Low-cost auto insurance—intended to decrease the number of uninsured drivers by making minimal liability coverage available at a reduced cost.

    b. No pay, no play law—prohibits uninsured drivers from initiating lawsuits for noneconomic damages, such as pain and suffering.

    c. Unsatisfied judgment funds—provide injured persons compensation for judgments that cannot be collected against negligent drivers.

D. Uninsured motorists (UM) coverage compensates an insured for bodily injury caused by an uninsured motorist, a hit-and-run driver, or a driver whose insurer is insolvent. Most states require that all automobile liability policies contain UM coverage unless the insured voluntarily waives the coverage in writing.

  1. Advantage—It provides some financial protection against uninsured drivers.

   2. Disadvantages
      a. Unless the insured has purchased higher UM limits, the maximum paid for a bodily injury claim is limited to the state's financial responsibility or compulsory insurance law requirement.
      b. To collect, an injured person must establish the uninsured motorist's legal responsibility for the accident, which can be difficult and may involve legal proceedings.
      c. Property damage is excluded in many states and optional in others.
      d. The victim is paying for insurance to protect against the failure of others to act responsibly.

E. Underinsured motorists (UIM) coverage provides additional limits of protection to the victim of an auto accident when the negligent driver's insurance limits are insufficient to pay for the damages.
   1. Advantage—UIM assists in compensating auto accident victims who would not be fully compensated otherwise.
   2. Disadvantage—Even the underinsured coverage may be insufficient to cover all costs. Also, the victim is paying for insurance to protect against the failure of others to act responsibly and to carry sufficient liability limits.

F. No-fault automobile insurance—Many states have no-fault auto insurance laws that restrict the filing of lawsuits against at-fault drivers.
   1. Under a no-fault system, an injured person does not need to establish fault and prove negligence in order to collect payment for damages.
   2. Certain no-fault laws place some restrictions on an injured person's right to sue a negligent driver who causes an accident. In some states, when a claim is below a certain monetary threshold, the injured motorist collects for injuries under his or her own insurance policy.
   3. No-fault laws were developed to avoid the costly and time-consuming process of determining legal liability for auto accidents under the tort liability system.
   4. Because no-fault laws limit the number of lawsuits that result from auto accidents, the burden on the state's court system is reduced, as are overall costs.
   5. Advantages
      a. No-fault plans eliminate the need to determine fault.
      b. They eliminate inequities in claim payments. Under the tort liability system, small claims may be overpaid, and claims involving serious injuries may be underpaid.

c. They expand the limited scope of the tort system, under which many persons injured, or the beneficiaries of those killed, in auto accidents do not collect or collect less than their full economic loss.

d. They decrease the proportion of premium dollars used for claim investigation and legal costs.

e. They reduce delays in payments. Many claims take months or even years to settle under the tort liability system.

6. Disadvantages

a. Auto insurance premiums have not decreased significantly and, in some cases, have increased in states that have implemented no-fault plans.

b. The rating system used for no-fault insurance may unfairly allocate accident costs to the drivers who are not responsible for the accidents, thus increasing premiums for good drivers.

c. No-fault benefits do not include payment for pain and suffering.

d. In states with stated monetary thresholds, some physicians, lawyers, and other professionals abuse the system by inflating fees charged for services or charging for unnecessary services and procedures. These actions lead to higher auto insurance costs for all policyholders.

Educational Objective 2

Describe no-fault automobile laws in terms of each of the following:

- **Types of no-fault laws**

- **Benefits required by no-fault laws**

Key Points:

A. No-fault laws authorize or mandate auto no-fault insurance, often referred to as personal injury protection (PIP), and they define the benefits that insurers can or must provide. Thus, insurers in no-fault states often avoid the costly and time-consuming process of determining legal responsibility for auto accidents and instead handle claims quickly so that injured persons can be compensated for their medical expenses and lost wages.

B. Types of No-Fault Laws
  1. Pure no-fault—Under pure no-fault, an injured person would not need to establish fault and prove negligence in order to collect payment for damages, regardless of the injury's severity. A pure no-fault system would abolish use of the tort liability system for bodily injuries resulting from auto accidents. No state has yet enacted a pure no-fault law.
  2. Modified no-fault plans—Modified no-fault plans place some restrictions on the right to sue an at-fault driver but do not entirely eliminate the right.
    a. Under a modified no-fault plan, injured motorists collect economic losses (such as medical expenses and lost wages) from their own insurers through PIP benefits mandated by the plan.
    b. After collecting economic losses through their no-fault coverage, injured persons can sue at-fault drivers for any economic losses that exceed the no-fault coverage limits.
    c. Injured motorists can sue at-fault drivers for noneconomic losses (such as pain and suffering, emotional distress, and disfigurement) if their injuries exceed a threshold stated in the law. The threshold can be either a monetary threshold (also called a dollar threshold) or a verbal threshold.
      - When a monetary threshold applies, an injured motorist (or his or her survivors) can sue for noneconomic losses if the economic losses exceed a stated dollar amount.

- When a verbal threshold applies, an injured motorist (or his or her survivors) can sue for noneconomic losses if his or her injuries meet a verbal description of serious injuries. Examples of these injuries include death, permanent disfigurement or scarring, significant and permanent loss of a bodily function, and significant and permanent injury.

3. Add-on plans—An add-on plan adds no-fault benefits to auto insurance policies. It differs from a modified no-fault plan because it places no restrictions on the injured person's right to sue a negligent party for damages. An add-on plan offers the insured the option of collecting for economic losses through his or her own insurer.

4. Choice no-fault plans—Under a choice no-fault plan, when an auto insurance policy is purchased or renewed, the insured can choose whether to be covered on a modified no-fault basis or not. In most states with choice no-fault plans, insureds who choose not to be covered on a modified no-fault basis must purchase add-on no-fault coverages.

   a. The modified no-fault option provides premium reductions in return for limitations on the right to sue for damages for certain types of auto injuries.

   b. If modified no-fault coverage is not selected, the insured retains full rights to seek compensation from the negligent party, but the insurer charges a higher premium.

C. Benefits Required by No-Fault Laws—Benefits required by no-fault laws typically include medical expenses, rehabilitation expenses, loss of earnings, expenses for essential services, funeral expenses, and survivors' loss benefits.

1. Insurers provide no-fault benefits by adding an endorsement to an auto insurance policy, typically called a PIP endorsement (or, in some states, "basic reparations"). The coverage provided by no-fault insurance is called PIP coverage.

2. Nearly all no-fault laws specify coverage only for bodily injury and exclude property damage.

3. Some states require that insurers offer (for an additional premium) optional higher benefits than the minimum prescribed by no-fault laws. Additionally, some states require insurers to provide optional deductibles, allowing insureds to reduce or eliminate certain no-fault benefits for a reduced premium.

4. No-fault laws typically allow the no-fault insurer to collect payment (through subrogation) from at-fault parties to the extent that no-fault benefits were paid. Often, the insurer can require reimbursement of benefits it has paid to the insured if the insured subsequently recovers from the responsible party through legal action.

Educational Objective 3
Explain how high-risk drivers may obtain auto insurance.

Key Points:

For drivers who cannot obtain insurance from private insurers in the voluntary market, states have created mechanisms to make insurance available in a residual market (also called the shared market).

A. Voluntary Market Programs

1. High-risk drivers include those who habitually violate traffic laws; those who have been responsible for an excessive number of traffic accidents; and those who have been convicted of certain serious offenses, such as reckless driving, driving with a suspended license, or driving under the influence of alcohol or drugs. Some insurers in the voluntary market offer insurance programs for high-risk drivers. These voluntary insurers accept their own applications, service their policies, pay their claims and expenses, and retain full responsibility for their underwriting results.

2. Insurance in high-risk driver programs generally has several common characteristics, including the following:

    a. In many cases, private insurers limit coverage amounts to those that comply with the state's financial responsibility or compulsory insurance requirement. In some cases, private insurers offer optional higher limits.

    b. Medical payments coverage may be limited.

    c. Collision insurance may be available only with a high deductible.

    d. Premiums are substantially higher than premiums charged for average and above-average drivers.

B. Residual Market Programs—States have developed various programs for high-risk drivers in the residual market, including the following:

1. Automobile insurance plans (also called assigned risk plans)

    a. Under a state's automobile insurance plan, all auto insurers doing business in the state are assigned their proportionate share of high-risk drivers based on the total volume of auto insurance written in the state.

    b. State automobile insurance plans usually have the following common characteristics:

- Applicants must show that they have been unable to obtain auto liability insurance within a certain number of days (usually sixty) of the application.
- The minimum limits of insurance offered are at least equal to the state's financial responsibility or compulsory insurance requirement.
- Certain applicants may be ineligible for coverage.
- Premiums are generally higher than premiums in the voluntary market.

2. Joint underwriting associations (JUAs)

    a. Several states have established joint underwriting associations (JUAs), which set the insurance rates and approve the policy forms to be used for high-risk drivers. Although JUAs vary by state, generally, a limited number of insurers are designated as servicing insurers to handle high-risk business.

    b. Agents and brokers submit applications of high-risk drivers to the JUA or to a designated servicing insurer. The servicing insurer usually receives applications, issues policies, collects premiums, settles claims, and provides other necessary services.

    c. In a state that offers a JUA, all auto insurers pay a proportionate share of total underwriting losses and expenses based on each insurer's share of voluntary auto insurance written in the state, a portion of which can be used to compensate the servicing insurers.

3. Other programs

    a. Reinsurance facility

- Under this pool arrangement, insurers accept all auto insurance applicants who have a valid driver's license; the insurers issue policies, collect premiums, and settle claims. However, if an applicant for auto insurance is considered a high-risk driver, the insurer has the option of assigning the driver's premiums and losses to the reinsurance facility while continuing to service the policy.
- All auto insurers doing business in the state share any underwriting losses and the expenses of the reinsurance facility in proportion to the total auto insurance that they write in that state.

b. State fund mechanism

One state, Maryland, has established a state fund mechanism that provides insurance to high-risk applicants. The state requires all private insurers to subsidize any losses, but the insurers can recover losses by surcharging their insureds.

Educational Objective 4

Describe automobile insurance rate regulation in terms of each of the following:

- **Rating factors**
- **Matching price to exposure**
- **Competition**
- **Other regulatory issues**

Key Points:

State rating laws generally require insurers to use rates that are adequate to pay all claims and expenses, reasonable (not excessive) for the exposure presented, and not unfairly discriminatory.

A. Rating Factors

1. Primary rating factors—Most states and insurers use primary rating factors for determining the cost of personal auto insurance. Several states no longer permit the use of some factors that they consider unfairly discriminatory. Primary rating factors include the following:

   a. Territory—Determined by where the auto is normally used and garaged, each of which affects the frequency and severity of auto accidents.

   b. Use of the auto—The auto's principal use classification reflects accident statistics. Typical use categories include pleasure, driving to work or school, business, and farm.

   c. Age—Young drivers have less driving experience and tend to be involved in accidents more frequently than older drivers; younger drivers' rates are often higher than more experienced drivers' rates.

   d. Gender—Women have tended to have fewer accidents than men in the same age categories, particularly among youthful drivers, so rates are often lower for women than for men; however, this tendency is changing.

   e. Marital status—Young married men tend to have fewer accidents than young unmarried men, and rates often reflect this tendency.

2. Other rating factors—Personal auto insurers often use the following additional rating factors, which are not essential in determining rating classifications:

   a. Driving record—Almost all insurers use an applicant's driving record to determine whether the individual presents an acceptable exposure and, if so, at what rate.

   b. Driver education—A premium discount may be provided for young drivers who complete an approved driver education course. Some insurers offer premium discounts to drivers age fifty-five and older who successfully complete defensive driver training courses. Driver training can help reduce the frequency and severity of auto losses.

   c. Good student—Students who maintain good grades may be offered premium discounts because, theoretically, they have fewer accidents than poor or average students.

   d. Multi-car policy—Most insurers give a multi-car discount when more than one auto is insured under the same policy. This discount is based on the assumption that two or more autos owned by the same insured will not be driven as often as a single auto. Additionally, it is less costly for the insurer to cover additional autos under the same contract, so savings may be passed to the insured.

   e. Years of driving experience—Generally, drivers with more years of experience have fewer accidents.

   f. Credit-based insurance score—Some insurers consider an applicant's insurance score. This numerical ranking is based on information from an individual's financial history. Actuarial research indicates that insureds with low insurance scores submit more claims than insureds with high insurance scores.

   g. Type of auto—The performance, age, and damageability of an auto can affect the rates for physical damage coverage on it.

   h. Deductibles—Insureds who choose higher deductibles for collision and other physical damage coverage on their autos can receive a credit because they retain a portion of covered losses.

   i. Liability limits—Rates are generally based on the minimum liability limits required by the state, and premiums increase if the insured chooses higher limits.

3. Other discounts and credits—Some insurers give discounts or credits for automobile features or practices of the insured that reduce insurer costs.

   a. Anti-theft devices can reduce the frequency of theft losses.

  b. Passive restraints (airbags) can reduce the severity of injuries.

  c. Reduced auto use by a student who attends a school that is more than a specified distance from home and does not garage an insured auto at school can reduce the frequency of losses.

  d. Having more than one type of policy with the same insurer reduces administrative costs.

  e. Multiple years of continuous coverage with the insurer reduces acquisition costs.

B. Matching Price to Exposure

 1. Insurers often divide auto insurance applicants into homogeneous classes, or rating categories, such as "preferred," "standard," and "nonstandard," that reflect different levels of exposure to loss.

 2. Applicants with good driving records and rating factors that suggest they present minimal loss exposure are categorized as preferred.

 3. Applicants with poor driving records or rating factors that suggest they present greater loss exposure are categorized as nonstandard and are charged higher rates.

 4. Usually insurers have a standard rating category for drivers who fall between these two extremes and present an average loss exposure.

 5. Regulators usually approve these rating categories because policyholders receive equitable treatment based on the loss exposures they present.

C. Competition

 1. Insurers cannot decrease rates to the point at which they can no longer cover the costs of claims and expenses. In times of high underwriting losses and low profits, insurers must raise rates, restrict the number and types of new applicants they will accept, or take other steps to become more profitable.

 2. Because insurers tend to consider competitive cycles in pricing personal auto insurance, regulators monitor rates carefully to ensure adequacy and reasonableness.

  a. Insurance regulators monitor rates primarily through rate filings.

  b. Insurers' rates must always meet the state requirements

D. Other Regulatory Issues

   1. Rising healthcare costs

      a. Increases in automobile insurance rates can often be linked to that portion of the premium linked to healthcare costs.

      b. One component of auto insurance coverage is personal injury protection (PIP), which pays the healthcare bills for individuals injured in auto accidents.

      c. The increasing cost of healthcare in the U.S. directly impacts not only the medical payments/PIP side of premiums, but also liability payments and uninsured motorist coverage.

   2. Environmental issues

      a. These can affect auto insurance coverages and rates because automobiles are a primary source of pollution emissions.

      b. Most environmental laws affecting auto insurance are state regulations.

         • State emissions regulations increase auto costs and result in higher claim payments for more expensive autos.

         • California's "pay-as-you-drive" regulation enables insurers to offer consumers rates that are based on actual instead of estimated miles driven. This provides financial incentives to drive less.

   3. Vehicle modifications

      a. Such modifications as a lowered or raised suspension, increased engine size, and tinted windows can increase risk and insurance premiums because modifications can put insureds at a greater risk of collision.

      b. Even modifications that would appear to create safer vehicles, like improved brake systems, can increase insurance costs for several reasons:

         • Modifications can increase auto values and, as a result, insurers' claim payments.

         • Modified autos can attract thieves, also increasing insurers' claim payments.

         • Auto performance modifications improve auto performance, which can result in more severe accidents.

Key Words and Phrases:

Key Words

Financial responsibility laws
Laws enacted to ensure that motorists have the financial ability to pay for any property damage or bodily injury they might cause as a result of driving or owning an auto.

Compulsory auto insurance law
Law that requires the owners or operators of automobiles to carry automobile liability insurance at least equal to certain minimum limits before the vehicle can be licensed or registered.

First party
The insured in an insurance contract.

Unsatisfied judgment fund
A fund designed to provide a source of recovery for victims of motor vehicle accidents when an at-fault motorist is unable to pay any judgment.

Uninsured motorists (UM) coverage
Coverage that provides a source of recovery for occupants of a covered auto or for qualifying pedestrians who are injured in an accident caused by an at-fault motorist who does not have the state minimum liability insurance or by a hit-and-run driver.

Underinsured motorists (UIM) coverage
Coverage that applies when a negligent driver has liability insurance at the time of the accident but has limits lower than those of the injured person's coverage.

No-fault automobile insurance
Insurance that covers automobile accident victims on a first-party basis, allowing them to collect damages from their own insurers regardless of who was at fault.

No-fault laws
State statutes that require motorists to purchase (or require insurers to make available) insurance that provides minimum first-party benefits to injured persons regardless of fault.

Monetary threshold (dollar threshold)
In a no-fault system, a dollar limit in total medical expenses an injured victim must exceed before he or she is permitted to sue the other party.

Verbal threshold
In a no-fault system, the designated criteria that are verbally "set forth in the statute that limit the right to sue."

Add-on plan
In a no-fault system, a plan that provides certain personal injury protection (PIP)-type benefits such as medical payments and disability coverages to injured victims, without regard to fault.

Choice no-fault plan
In a no-fault system, a plan that gives the insured the option, at the time an auto insurance policy is purchased or renewed, of choosing whether to be covered on a no-fault basis.

Personal injury protection (PIP) coverage
Coverage that pays benefits, regardless of fault, for medical expense, income loss, and other benefits, resulting from bodily injury to occupants of a covered auto.

Subrogation
The process by which an insurer can, after it has paid a loss under the policy, recover the amount paid from any party (other than the insured) who caused the loss or is otherwise legally liable for the loss.

Residual market
The term referring collectively to insurers and other organizations that make insurance available through a shared risk mechanism to those who cannot obtain coverage in the admitted market.

Safe driver insurance plan (SDIP)
Plan that allows for lower basic premiums for accident-free driving records and a surcharge for accidents.

Automobile insurance plan
Plan for insuring high-risk drivers in which all auto insurers doing business in the state are assigned their proportionate share of such drivers based on the total volume of auto insurance written in the state.

Joint underwriting association (JUA)
Organization that designates servicing insurers to handle high-risk auto insurance business; all auto insurers in the state are assessed a proportionate share of the losses and expenses based on their percentage of the voluntary auto insurance premiums written in the state.

Reinsurance facility
A state-wide reinsurance pool to which insurers can assign premiums and losses for high-risk drivers; original insurers service the policies, but all insurers in the pool share the losses and expenses of the facility in proportion to the total auto insurance they write in that state.

Personal Auto Policy: Liability, Med Pay, and UM Coverage

Educational Objective 1
Summarize the sections of the Personal Auto Policy.

Key Points:

Many auto owners in the United States use some form of the Insurance Services Office's (ISO's) Personal Auto Policy (PAP) to insure their personal auto loss exposures. The ISO PAP consists of a Declarations page, an Agreement and Definitions page, and six separate sections. Almost all PAPs also include one or more endorsements.

Study Tips

Have you contacted The Institutes to schedule an exam?

A. Declarations

The Declarations page includes general information:

   1. The name and mailing address of the insured

   2. The name of the insurer issuing the policy and the name and address of the producer, if applicable

   3. The policy period, a description of the covered autos, limits of liability, premium and rating information, and any endorsements that may apply to the policy

B. Agreement and Definitions

The Agreement and Definitions page includes a general agreement stating that the insurer is providing the coverage subject to payment of premium and to the terms of the policy.

C. Overview of Coverages

   1. Part A—Liability Coverage protects the insured against claims or lawsuits for bodily injury or property damage arising out of the operation of an auto.

   2. Part B—Medical Payments Coverage compensates for reasonable and necessary medical and funeral expenses because of bodily injury to the insured caused by an auto accident.

   3. Part C—Uninsured Motorists Coverage pays damages if an insured is injured by an uninsured motorist, a hit-and-run driver, or a driver whose insurer is insolvent.

4. Part D—Coverage for Damage to Your Auto compensates for physical damage to a covered auto and to certain nonowned autos. Also referred to as physical damage coverage, Part D includes other than collision and collision coverages.

5. Part E—Duties After an Accident or Loss outlines the duties required of an insured after an accident or a loss, such as requirements for notifying the insurer of the details of any losses that happen.

6. Part F—General Provisions contains information such as how changes to the policy can be made, provisions for cancellation and termination of the policy, and descriptions of the policy period and territory.

D. Endorsements

1. In addition to the PAP coverage form, the policy also includes state-specific endorsements usually used to adapt the PAP to state-specific laws and regulations applying to auto insurance.

2. Endorsements are also available to provide additional coverages that are desired by some policyholders but are not purchased by all policyholders. These endorsements are separate from the PAP coverage form but must be considered as part of the overall structure of a PAP.

▶▶

Educational Objective 2

Identify the types of information typically contained on the declarations page of a personal auto policy.

Key Points:

Most insurance policies contain a declarations page that provides basic information about the parties involved and the specific coverage provided.

A. Insurer—The name of the insurer providing the coverage. If an agency or brokerage sold the policy, its name and contact information may also be included.

B. Named Insured—The name and mailing address of the policyholder or named insured. This is the party that is responsible for premium payment, can request cancellation of the policy, and receives any notices issued by the insurer.

C. Policy Period—The time during which the policy provides coverage.

D. Description of Insured Autos—Identification of each the autos and trailers specifically insured under the policy.
   1. This description usually includes each vehicle's year, make, model, and vehicle identification number (VIN).
   2. It may also include body type, annual mileage, use of the vehicle, date of purchase, or other information about each vehicle.

E. Schedule of Coverages—Indication of the coverages and limits that apply to each listed auto, along with the premium for each coverage. If Part D—Coverage for Damage to Your Auto applies, the deductibles are also shown separately for other than collision coverage and for collision coverage.

F. Applicable Endorsements–List of any endorsements that are attached to the policy. Most policies will also include at least one state-specific endorsement.

G. Lienholder—Whether it is owned or leased, a vehicle may be financed through a bank, savings and loan association, credit union, or other organization that holds the title to the vehicle until the loan is paid. In such a case, the name of the lender, loss payee, or lienholder is usually shown on the Declarations page.

H. Garage Location—If an insured auto will be kept garaged primarily at a location other than the at insured's mailing address stated on the Declarations page, that separate location will also be listed in the declarations.

I. Rating Information—The rating class for the vehicle and any applicable credits and discounts may be shown.

J. Signature—The signature of an authorized legal representative of the insurer is usually shown at the bottom of the Declarations page. Also included is the countersignature date, which is the date when the policy was signed by the authorized legal representative.

Educational Objective 3
Define the words and phrases included in the Definitions section of the Personal Auto Policy.

Key Points:

A. You and your—These words refer to the named insured shown on the PAP Declarations page as well as an unnamed spouse of the named insured—provided that the spouse is a resident of the same household.

    1. An unnamed spouse who moves out of the household but remains married to the insured is considered "you" for another ninety days or until the policy expires—whichever comes first.

    2. Coverage ceases if the spouse is named on another policy.

B. We, us, and our—Refer to the insurer providing insurance under the contract, generally the company named in the declarations.

C. Leased vehicle—A leased private passenger auto, pickup, or van is deemed to be an owned auto if it is leased under a written agreement for a continuous period of at least six months.

D. Bodily injury—Bodily harm, sickness, or disease, including death.

E. Business—Includes a trade, a profession, or an occupation.

F. Family member—A person who is related to the named insured or spouse by blood, marriage, or adoption and who resides in the named insured's household. This definition also includes a ward or a foster child.

G. Occupying—In, upon, getting in, on, out, or off.

H. Property damage—Physical injury to, destruction of, or loss of use of tangible property.

I. Trailer—A vehicle designed to be pulled by a private passenger auto, a pickup, or a van, including a farm wagon or farm implement towed by a vehicle included in the definition of a trailer.

J. Your covered auto—Applies to the vehicles that are covered under the PAP and includes the following four classes of vehicles:

    1. Any vehicle shown in the declarations.

    2. A newly acquired auto.

    3. Any trailer you own.

4. A temporary substitute auto or trailer—A vehicle that is used as a short-term substitute for another covered auto that is out of normal use due to breakdown, repair, servicing, loss, or destruction. These vehicles are covered under all PAP coverages except damage to your auto (physical damage) which treats them the same as other nonowned autos.

K. Newly Acquired Auto

1. Includes the following types of vehicles that become an owned vehicle during the policy period:

   a. A private passenger auto

   b. A pick up or van—Certain weight and usage restrictions apply.

2. For all PAP coverages except physical damage coverage, a newly acquired auto automatically receives coverage equal to the broadest coverage indicated for any vehicle shown in the declarations.

   a. An additional auto is automatically covered for fourteen days after the named insured becomes the owner. The insured must request coverage beyond fourteen days.

   b. A replacement auto is covered for the remainder of the policy period, even if the insured does not ask for coverage.

3. For physical damage coverage, an insured who carries collision coverage or other than collision (OTC) coverage on at least one auto receives automatic coverage on a newly acquired auto for fourteen days. The coverage is equal to the broadest coverage (that is, that with the smallest deductible) on any vehicle currently shown in the policy declarations.

   a. An insured who does not have these coverages on at least one auto receives automatic physical damage coverage on a newly acquired auto for four days, subject to a $500 deductible.

   b. In either case, the insured must ask the insurer to add the auto to the policy within the automatic coverage period in order to extend coverage beyond the period.

Educational Objective 4

Summarize each of the provisions in Part A—Liability Coverage of the Personal Auto Policy.

Key Points:

Part A—Liability Coverage consists of the following provisions: Insuring Agreement, Supplementary Payments, Exclusions, Limit of Liability, Out of State Coverage, Financial Responsibility, and Other Insurance.

A. The Part A Insuring Agreement states the insurer's duty to pay damages and defense costs and defines the persons and organizations insured under Part A.

   1. Damages Covered—The insurer agrees to pay compensatory and punitive damages for bodily injury or property damage for which an insured is legally responsible because of an auto accident.

   2. Defense Costs Covered—In addition to the limit of liability the insurer agrees to pay legal costs incurred to defend the insured in a liability suit and prejudgment interest.

   3. Persons and Organizations Insured—Part A provides liability coverage for the following four classes of persons or organizations:

      a. The named insured and family members, covered for the ownership, maintenance, or use of any auto or trailer, including covered autos borrowed autos, rented vehicles (autos or trucks), or any other auto, subject to the policy exclusions

      b. Any person using the named insured's covered auto, as defined in the PAP

      c. Any person or organization legally responsible for the acts of a covered person while using a covered auto

      d. Any person or organization legally responsible for the named insured's or family member's use of any automobile or trailer, provided that the person or organization does not own or hire the auto or trailer

B. Part A lists five supplementary payments that do not reduce the limit of liability:

1. Cost of bail bonds—The insurer agrees to pay up to $250 for the cost of bail bonds (bail bond premiums) required because of an accident that results in bodily injury or property damage covered by the policy.

2. Premiums on appeal bonds and bonds to release attachments.

3. Interest accruing after a judgment (postjudgment interest).

4. Loss of earnings up to $200 because of the insured's attendance at a hearing or trial at the insurer's request.

5. Other reasonable expenses incurred at the insurer's request.

C. Exclusions—PAP liability coverage is subject to the following exclusions:

1. Intentional bodily injury or property damage caused by the insured.

2. Property owned or transported by an insured.

3. Property rented to, used by, or in the care of the insured.

4. Bodily injury to an employee of an insured who is injured during the course of employment.

5. Insured's ownership or operation of a vehicle while it is being used as a public or livery conveyance. The exclusion does not apply to share-the-expense car pools.

6. Garage business use, that is, while the insured is employed or engaged in the business of selling, repairing, servicing, storing, or parking vehicles designed for use mainly on public highways.

7. Other business use, that is vehicles maintained or used in any business other than farming or ranching.

8. The insured's use of a vehicle without a reasonable belief that he or she is entitled to do so, except when another family member uses the owned auto of a named insured.

9. Nuclear energy liability losses, that is liability for bodily injury or property damage caused by an insured who is also covered by a nuclear energy liability policy.

10. Liability arising out of the ownership, maintenance, or use of vehicles with fewer than four wheels or designed for off-road use.

11. Other vehicles owned by the insured or available for the insured's regular use.

12. Vehicles owned by or available for any family member's regular use (other than covered autos). This exclusion does not apply to the named insured and spouse while maintaining or occupying such a vehicle.

13. Any vehicle that is located inside a racing facility for the purpose of preparing for, practicing for, or competing in any organized racing or speed contest.

D. Limit of Liability

    1. Most PAPs are written on a split-limits basis, with the three types of limits stated in the following order: bodily injury to each person, bodily injury to all persons in each accident, and property damage in each accident. Split limits of $100/$300/$50 mean that the insured has bodily injury liability limits of $100,000 per person and $300,000 for each accident, and a limit of $50,000 for property damage liability per accident.

    2. Some policies are written with a single limit that applies per accident to the total of both bodily injury and property damage liability. The Single Liability Limit endorsement modifies the policy to provide coverage on a single-limit basis.

    3. No one is entitled to receive duplicate payments for the same elements of loss under Part A—Liability Coverage, Part B—Medical Payments Coverage, Part C—Uninsured Motorists Coverage, or any underinsured motorists coverage provided by the policy.

E. Out of State Coverage—Applies when an auto accident occurs in a state other than the one in which the covered auto is principally garaged.

    1. If the accident occurs in a state that has a financial responsibility law or a similar law that requires higher liability limits than the limits shown in the declarations, the PAP automatically provides the higher required limits for that accident.

    2. If a state has a compulsory insurance law that requires nonresidents to maintain coverage whenever they use a vehicle in that state, the PAP provides the required minimum amounts and types of coverage.

F. Financial Responsibility—Many states' laws require insureds to demonstrate proof of financial responsibility after an accident or traffic violation has occurred.

    1. The PAP can be used to demonstrate proof of financial responsibility to the extent required by the state where the accident or traffic violation has occurred.

    2. If a financial responsibility law is changed to require higher minimum limits of liability, the PAP automatically complies with the new law.

G. Other Insurance—Addresses situations in which more than one auto policy covers a liability claim.

   1. If the insured has other applicable liability insurance on an owned vehicle, the insurer pays only its pro rata share of the loss. The insurer's share is the proportion of the loss that the limit of liability bears to the total of all applicable limits.

   2. If other liability insurance is available on a nonowned vehicle, including any vehicle used as a temporary substitute for a covered auto, the PAP coverage is excess over any other collectible insurance.

Educational Objective 5

Given a case describing an auto liability claim, determine whether Part A—Liability Coverage of the Personal Auto Policy would cover the claim and, if so, the amount the insurer would pay for the claim.

Key Points:

To adequately meet the requirements of this case study's educational objective, students should understand the DICE method of policy analysis as well as the specific policy forms and endorsements described in the case to make accurate coverage and loss settlement amount determinations.

Apply the steps in the DICE method to the specific issues of the coverage claim.

To determine whether a policy covers a loss, many insurance professionals apply the DICE method. ("DICE" is an acronym for categories of policy provisions: declarations, insuring agreement, conditions, and exclusions.) The DICE method has four steps:

1. Review of the declarations page to determine whether it covers the person or the property at the time of the loss

2. Review of the insuring agreement to determine whether it covers the loss

3. Review of policy conditions to determine compliance

4. Review of policy exclusions to determine whether they preclude coverage of the loss

Each of these four steps is used in every case. Other categories of policy provisions should be examined. For example, endorsements and terms defined in the policy should be reviewed in relation to the declarations, insuring agreement, exclusions, and conditions.

Educational Objective 6

Summarize each of the provisions in Part B—Medical Payments Coverage of the Personal Auto Policy.

Key Points:

Part B—Medical Payments Coverage of the Personal Auto Policy (PAP) includes the following provisions:

- Insuring Agreement
- Exclusions
- Limit of Liability
- Other Insurance

A. Insuring Agreement—States the insurer's promise to pay reasonable and necessary medical and funeral expenses incurred by an insured because of bodily injury caused by an accident.

1. The insurer agrees to pay only those expenses incurred for services rendered within three years from the date of the accident.

2. The types of expenses payable include those for medical, surgical, x-ray, dental, and funeral services.

3. Medical payments coverage applies without regard to fault.

4. The following two classes of insureds are covered under Part B:

   a. The named insured and "family members" (as defined in the PAP)—These individuals are covered for their medical expenses if they are injured while occupying a motor vehicle or as pedestrians when struck by a motor vehicle designed for use mainly on public roads.

   b. Any other person while occupying a covered auto—Medical expenses of passengers in a covered auto are covered.

B. Exclusions—Medical payments coverage does not apply to the following:

1. Injuries sustained by an insured while occupying a motorized vehicle with fewer than four wheels.

2. Injuries sustained by an insured while occupying a vehicle used as a public or livery conveyance (such as a taxi or public bus). This exclusion does not apply to share-the-expense car pools.

3. Injuries that occur while the vehicle is located for use as a residence or premises.

4. Injuries that occur during the course of employment if workers compensation benefits are required or available.

5. Injuries sustained by an insured while occupying, or when struck by, another vehicle owned by the insured or furnished or available for the insured's regular use.

6. Injuries sustained by an insured while occupying, or when struck by, a vehicle (other than a covered auto) owned by or furnished or available for family member's regular use. However, this exclusion does not apply to the named insured and spouse.

7. Injuries sustained by an insured while using a vehicle without a reasonable belief that he or she is entitled to do so. This exclusion does not apply to a "family member" (as defined) using a covered auto which is owned by the named insured or spouse.

8. Injuries sustained by an insured while occupying a vehicle used in the insured's business. This exclusion does not apply to a private passenger auto, a pickup or van, or a trailer used with these vehicles.

9. Bodily injury from nuclear weapons or war, including discharge of a nuclear weapon (even if accidental), insurrection, rebellion, or revolution.

10. Bodily injury caused by nuclear reaction, radiation, or radioactive contamination.

11. Bodily injury an insured sustains while occupying any vehicle that is located inside a racing facility for the purpose of preparing for, practicing for, or competing in any organized racing or speed contest.

C. Limit of Liability—The limit of insurance for medical payments coverage is stated in the declarations.

1. This limit, typically between $1,000 and $10,000, is the maximum amount that will be paid to each injured person in a single accident, regardless of the number of insured persons, claims made, vehicles or premiums shown on the policy, or vehicles involved in the auto accident.

2. No one is entitled to receive duplicate payments for the same elements of loss under Part B—Medical Payments Coverage, Part A—Liability Coverage, Part C—Uninsured Motorists Coverage, or any underinsured motorists coverage provided by the policy.

D. Other Insurance

1. If the medical payments coverage of more than one insurance policy applies to a claim, each insurer pays its pro rata share based on the proportion that its limit of liability bears to the total of applicable limits.

2. With respect to a nonowned vehicle or a vehicle while used as a temporary substitute for the insured's covered auto, medical payments coverage under a PAP is excess over any other collectible auto insurance that pays medical or funeral expenses.

▶▶

Educational Objective 7

Given a case describing an auto medical payments claim, determine whether Part B—Medical Payments Coverage of the Personal Auto Policy would cover the claim and, if so, the amount the insurer would pay for the claim.

Key Points:

To adequately meet the requirements of this case study's educational objective, students should understand the DICE method of policy analysis as well as the specific policy forms and endorsements described in the case to make accurate coverage and loss settlement amount determinations.

Apply the steps in the DICE method to the specific issues of the coverage claim.

To determine whether a policy covers a loss, many insurance professionals apply the DICE method. ("DICE" is an acronym for categories of policy provisions: declarations, insuring agreement, conditions, and exclusions.) The DICE method has four steps:

1. Review of the declarations page to determine whether it covers the person or the property at the time of the loss
2. Review of the insuring agreement to determine whether it covers the loss
3. Review of policy conditions to determine compliance
4. Review of policy exclusions to determine whether they preclude coverage of the loss

Each of these four steps is used in every case. Other categories of policy provisions should be examined. For example, endorsements and terms defined in the policy should be reviewed in relation to the declarations, insuring agreement, exclusions, and conditions.

Educational Objective 8

Summarize each of the provisions in Part C—Uninsured Motorists Coverage of the Personal Auto Policy.

Key Points:

Part C includes the following provisions: Insuring Agreement, Exclusions, Limit of Liability, Other Insurance, and Arbitration.

A. Insuring Agreement—The insurer agrees to pay compensatory damages that the insured is legally entitled to recover from the owner or operator of an uninsured motor vehicle because of bodily injury caused by an accident.

1. Damages could include medical expenses, rehabilitation expenses, and lost wages. Punitive or exemplary damages are not covered.

2. Some states' uninsured motorists (UM) coverage applies to property damage claims, subject to a deductible.

3. Insureds receive compensation without having to sue the uninsured driver. However, UM coverage applies only if the uninsured motorist is legally responsible for the accident.

4. The following three classes of persons are considered insureds under UM coverage:

   a. The named insured and family members while occupying a covered auto or a vehicle that they do not own. They are also covered as pedestrians.

   b. Any other person occupying a covered auto.

   c. Any person legally entitled to recover damages because of bodily injury to a person in the two previously described classes.

5. An uninsured motor vehicle is a land motor vehicle or trailer of any type that meets any of the following criteria:

   a. No bodily injury liability insurance or bond applies to the vehicle at the time of the accident.

   b. A bodily injury liability policy or bond is in force, but its limit of liability is less than the minimum required by the financial responsibility law in the state where the named insured's covered auto is principally garaged.

   c. The vehicle is a hit-and-run vehicle, whose operator or owner cannot be identified, that hits the named insured or any family member; a vehicle that the named insured or any family member is occupying; or the named insured's covered auto.

    d. A bodily injury liability policy or bond applies at the time of the accident, but the insurance or bonding company denies coverage or is insolvent.

    e. The definition of uninsured motor vehicle does not include vehicles available for the insured's regular use, a self-insurer (unless insolvent), or a government agency, or vehicles operated on rails or crawler threads, designed for use off public roads, or while located for use as a residence.

B. Exclusions

    1. Owned but not insured vehicle—Eliminates coverage for injuries sustained by an insured while occupying, or when struck by, any vehicle owned by that insured but not insured for UM under the policy.

    2. Owned vehicle with primary UM coverage in another policy—Eliminates coverage for injuries sustained in a vehicle owned by the named insured that has primary UM coverage under another policy.

    3. Claim settlement that prejudices insurer's right of recovery—Eliminates coverage of claims that the insured settles without the insurer's consent if such a settlement prejudices the insurer's right to recover payment.

    4. Public or livery conveyance—Eliminates coverage for injuries the insured suffers while occupying a covered auto when it is being used as a public or livery conveyance (such as a taxi or public bus). The exclusion does not apply to a share-the-expense car pool.

    5. Vehicle used without reasonable belief of being entitled—Eliminates coverage for injuries suffered by any person who uses a vehicle without a reasonable belief that he or she is entitled to do so. The exclusion does not apply to family members.

    6. No benefit to workers compensation or disability benefits insurer—Prevents workers compensation or disability benefits insurers from obtaining reimbursement under an injured worker's UM coverage for payments they have made for the same injuries.

    7. Punitive damages—UM coverage applies only to compensatory damages, which do not include punitive damages.

C. Limit of Liability—The minimum amount of UM coverage available under the PAP is set by the financial responsibility or compulsory insurance law of the state in which the insured auto is principally garaged. Higher limits can be purchased for an additional premium.

    1. UM coverage is normally written on a split-limits basis, but coverage on a single-limit basis is available by endorsement.

2. The UM section states that no person will receive duplicate payments for any loss under any other parts of the PAP.

3. The insurer will not make duplicate payment under the UM coverage if payment has been made by any other person or organization or if the injured person is entitled to workers compensation or disability benefits for the injuries.

D. Other Insurance—If other applicable UM insurance is available under one or more policies, the following provisions apply:

1. The total amount paid will be no more than the highest limit of any of the policies that provide coverage.

2. Coverage for an accident involving a vehicle the named insured does not own is provided on an excess basis over any collectible insurance providing coverage on a primary basis.

3. If more than one policy provides coverage on a primary basis, each insurer's share is equal to the proportion its UM limit bears to the total amount available under all applicable primary coverages.

4. If more than one policy provides coverage on an excess basis, each policy will contribute proportionally to the insured's recovery, based on the excess limits each policy provides.

E. Arbitration—If the insurer and insured cannot agree on whether the insured is entitled to recover damages from an uninsured motorist or on the amount of damages, the dispute can be settled by arbitration. However, arbitration does not include disputes involving coverage, such as whether a policy exclusion applies.

Educational Objective 9

Describe underinsured motorists insurance in terms of:

- **Its purpose**

- **The ways in which it can vary by state**

Key Points:

A. Underinsured motorists (UIM) coverage goes beyond uninsured motorists (UM) coverage. It is important in situations in which a negligent driver is insured for at least the minimum required financial responsibility limits but the policy's liability limits are insufficient to pay the insured's damages.

   1. In some states, the ISO Underinsured Motorists Coverage Endorsement (PP 03 11) can be added to the Personal Auto Policy (PAP) to supplement the UM coverage.

   2. In several states, however, insurers use either a state-specific UIM endorsement or a single, state-specific endorsement providing both UM and UIM coverages that replaces the UM coverage of the standard PAP.

B. States' UM/UIM statutes govern who is protected and under what circumstances, regardless of the policy provisions used by an insurer.

   1. Where the insured's vehicle is registered or principally garaged determines which state's laws apply.

   2. Some states mandate that UIM coverage be provided on all auto liability policies.

   3. Other states allow insureds to reject UIM coverage, but typically only if the named insured rejects the coverage in writing.

   4. Mandatory or optional limits for UIM coverage also vary by state.

      a. Many states require that the UIM limit equal the UM coverage limit, which, for many states, must also equal the PAP's bodily injury liability limit.

      b. In some states, the UM limit can be reduced, but not below the state's minimum financial responsibility limit.

5. States' UIM endorsements contain a "trigger," that is, something that must occur or exist in order for coverage to apply.

   a. Some states use a "limits trigger," applying the UIM endorsement when the negligent driver carries liability limits below the limits provided by the UIM coverage of the injured party.

   b. Other states use a "damages trigger," applying the UIM endorsement when the negligent driver carries liability insurance limits that are lower than the injured party's actual damages.

6. Another UIM variation among states relates to stacking, which is the application of two or more limits to a single auto accident.

   a. Stacking may involve two or more separate policies (interpolicy stacking). The UIM policy limit of one policy would be added to (stacked on) the UIM limit of the other policy. Some states allow interpolicy stacking by endorsement.

   b. Stacking can also occur within a single policy that covers more than one vehicle (intrapolicy stacking). Some states allow intrapolicy stacking by endorsement.

   c. In some states, the insured can choose between stacking or nonstacking but must pay a higher premium for a policy that allows stacking.

   d. Other states prohibit intrapolicy stacking. They require that the maximum to be paid for an accident is the single (unstacked) UIM limit shown on the Declarations page, regardless of the number of insureds, claims made, vehicles or premiums shown on the Declarations page, or vehicles involved.

Educational Objective 10

Given a case describing an uninsured motorists claim, determine whether Part C—Uninsured Motorists Coverage of the Personal Auto Policy would cover the claim and, if so, the amount the insurer would pay for the claim.

Key Points:

To adequately meet the requirements of this case study's educational objective, students should understand the DICE method of policy analysis, as well as the specific policy forms and endorsements described in the case, to make accurate coverage and loss settlement amount determinations.

Apply the steps in the DICE method to the specific issues of the coverage claim.

To determine whether a policy covers a loss, many insurance professionals apply the DICE method. ("DICE" is an acronym for categories of policy provisions: declarations, insuring agreement, conditions, and exclusions.) The DICE method has four steps:

1. Review of the declarations page to determine whether it covers the person or the property at the time of the loss
2. Review of the insuring agreement to determine whether it covers the loss
3. Review of policy conditions to determine compliance
4. Review of policy exclusions to determine whether they preclude coverage of the loss

Each of these four steps is used in every case. Other categories of policy provisions should be examined. For example, endorsements and terms defined in the policy should be reviewed in relation to the declarations, insuring agreement, exclusions, and conditions.

Key Words and Phrases:

Named insured
A person, corporation, partnership, or other entity identified as an insured party in an insurance policy's declarations page.

Policy period
The time frame, beginning with the inception date, during which insurance coverage applies.

Vehicle identification number (VIN)
A unique number that is assigned to each vehicle and that identifies certain vehicle characteristics.

Collision coverage
Coverage for direct and accidental loss or damage to a covered auto caused by collision with another object or by overturn.

Other than collision (OTC) coverage
Coverage for physical damage to a covered auto resulting from any cause of loss except collision or a cause of loss specifically excluded.

Compensatory damages
A payment awarded by a court to reimburse a victim for actual harm.

Split-limits basis
Separate coverage limits that allow one limit for bodily injury to each person; a second usually higher limit for bodily injury to all persons in each accident; and a third limit for all property damage in each accident.

Single-limits basis
One coverage limit that applies to all damages arising from bodily injury or property damage or both, resulting from a single accident.

Prejudgment interest
Interest that may accrue on damages before a judgment has been rendered.

Supplementary payments
Various expenses the insurer agrees to pay under a liability insurance policy (in addition to the liability limits) for items such as premiums on bail bonds and appeal bonds, loss of the insured's earnings because of attendance at trials, and other reasonable expenses incurred by the insured at the insurer's request.

Attachment
The act of seizing property to secure a judgment.

Postjudgment interest
Interest that may accrue on damages after a judgment has been entered in a court and before the money is paid.

Public or livery conveyance
In case law, a method of transportation that is indiscriminately offered to the general public, such as a taxi or public bus.

Uninsured motor vehicles
A land motor vehicle or trailer that is not insured for bodily injury liability, is insured for less than the financial responsibility limits, is a hit-and-run vehicle, or whose insurer denies coverage or becomes insolvent.

Arbitration
An alternative dispute resolution (ADR) method by which disputing parties use a neutral outside party to examine the issues and develop a settlement, which can be final and binding.

PAP: Physical Damage, Duties After an Accident, Endorsements

4

Educational Objective 1

Summarize each of the provisions in Part D—Coverage for Damage to Your Auto of the Personal Auto Policy.

Key Points:

Part D of the Personal Auto Policy (PAP) is a way to protect an insured's investment in a vehicle and includes these provisions:

A. In the Part D Insuring Agreement provision, the insurer promises to pay for any direct and accidental loss to "your covered auto" or a "non-owned auto" minus a deductible. Direct and accidental losses to an auto fall into two categories.

1. Collision losses—The PAP defines "collision" as the upset of or impact of "your covered auto" or a "non-owned auto" with another vehicle or object.

   a. Collision losses are paid regardless of fault.

   b. An insurer that pays an insured for collision losses has the right to recover payment from the driver who caused the accident through subrogation.

2. Other than collision losses (OTC)—OTC coverage insures auto physical damage losses that are not caused by collision and are not specifically excluded in the policy.

   a. Many motorists purchase only OTC coverage because it is less expensive than collision coverage and because it often has a lower deductible than that of collision coverage.

   b. The PAP does not specifically define OTC but does list certain causes of loss that are considered OTC, such as falling objects, fire, theft, explosion, wind, vandalism, contact with a bird or animal, and glass breakage.

   c. Any "direct and accidental loss" that is not due to collision and is not specifically excluded would be covered as an OTC loss.

3. Nonowned autos are also covered in Part D.

   a. An insured can occasionally drive a rented or borrowed auto, and the insured's physical damage insurance will cover the vehicle.

Study Tips

Are you interested in joining a formal class on this material? Go to our Web site, www.TheInstitutes.org, for a complete listing of public classes.

    b. However, if the insured regularly drives a rented or borrowed vehicle, or if one is made available for an insured's regular use, the insured's coverage does not apply.

  4. Part D requires deductibles for three reasons: to reduce small claims, to hold down premiums, and to encourage insureds to be careful in protecting their cars against damage or theft.

    a. A deductible of $100 or higher, specified in the policy declarations, typically applies to each covered collision loss.

    b. A separate deductible applies to OTC losses.

B. Under the Transportation Expenses provision, following a covered physical damage loss to a covered auto, the insurer will reimburse the insured for temporary transportation expenses, such as auto rental fees or taxi fares, up to $20 per day, to a maximum of $600 for each covered loss.

  1. The same limits apply to a nonowned auto when the insured is legally responsible to the auto's owner for the owner's transportation expenses.

  2. A nonowned rental car is also subject to these limits when the car's owner claims a loss of income because the car cannot be rented while it is being repaired and the named insured is legally responsible for the renter's loss of income.

  3. Transportation expenses coverage applies only to expenses incurred when the cause of loss is covered by the policy.

  4. Transportation expenses are not subject to a dollar-amount deductible. However, they are subject to a waiting period.

    a. A forty-eight-hour waiting period applies to total theft losses under OTC coverage.

    b. A twenty-four-hour waiting period applies to loss by other perils under both collision and OTC.

C. The Exclusions provision narrows Part D's broad coverage. There are thirteen exclusions:

  1. Physical damage insurance does not apply while the vehicle is used as a public or livery conveyance, such as a taxi or a bus. This exclusion does not apply to a share-the-expense car pool.

  2. Damage "due and confined to" wear and tear, freezing, mechanical or electrical breakdown or failure, and road damage to tires is excluded. This exclusion does not apply if the damage results from the total theft of a covered auto or a nonowned auto.

  3. Loss due to radioactive contamination, discharge of a nuclear weapon, war (declared or undeclared), civil war, insurrection, rebellion, or revolution is excluded.

4. Loss to any electronic equipment that reproduces, receives, or transmits audio, visual, or data signals is excluded. This exclusion does not apply to electronic equipment that is permanently installed in "your covered auto" or a nonowned auto.

5. Tapes, records, disks, and other media used with sound, video, or data equipment are not part of the auto and are therefore not covered under the PAP.

6. The PAP excludes coverage for a total loss to a covered auto or nonowned auto due to destruction or confiscation by governmental or civil authorities. This exclusion does not apply to the interests of any loss payees (such as banks or other lending institutions) in the covered auto.

7. Physical damage loss to a trailer, camper, or motor home that is not shown in the declarations is excluded. This exclusion does not apply to nonowned trailers and to camper bodies or trailers acquired during the policy period if insurance is requested within fourteen days after the insurer becomes the owner.

8. The PAP excludes physical damage coverage for loss to a nonowned auto when it is used by the insured or a family member who does not reasonably believe that he or she is entitled to use it.

9. Loss to equipment designed to detect police radar or laser beams is excluded.

10. Coverage is excluded for loss to any custom furnishings or equipment in or on any pickup or van. This exclusion does not apply to pickup caps, covers, or bedliners.

11. Also excluded is loss to a nonowned auto maintained or used in the business of selling, repairing, servicing, storing, or parking vehicles.

12. Loss to a covered auto or a nonowned auto is excluded if the auto is damaged while located in a facility designed for racing if the auto is being used to prepare for, practice for, or compete in any prearranged racing or speed contest.

13. If an insured's PAP provides physical damage coverage for an owned auto, the policy also provides physical damage coverage for a rental vehicle. However, the coverage is excluded if the rental agreement includes a damage waiver or if applicable state law precludes the rental company from recovering from the insured for the loss.

D. The Limit of Liability provision limits an insurer's liability for a physical damage loss to a covered auto.

  1. The insurer's liability is the lower of either the actual cash value (ACV) of the damaged or stolen property or the amount necessary to repair or replace the property with other property of like kind and quality.

  2. To determine ACV, an adjustment is made for depreciation and physical condition of the damaged property.

  3. When a vehicle sustains only a partial loss, the insurer usually pays the cost of repairing it, less any applicable deductible.

  4. However, if the damage to the vehicle is extensive and the cost of repairs exceeds the vehicle's ACV, the car may be declared a total loss. In such a case, the amount the insurer will pay is limited to the ACV of the damaged vehicle, less any applicable deductible.

  5. The insurer's maximum obligation is limited to $1,000 for electronic equipment that reproduces, receives, or transmits audio, visual or data signals and that is permanently installed, but not in the locations used by the original manufacturer of the auto.

  6. The maximum amount paid for a physical damage to a non-owned trailer is $1,500.

E. The Payment of Loss provision allows the insurer the option of paying for the loss in money or repairing or replacing the damaged or stolen property.

  1. If a stolen auto is returned to the insured, the insurer pays the cost to return it and also pays for any damage resulting from the theft.

  2. However, the insurer has the right to keep all or part of the stolen property and pay the insured an agreed or appraised value

F. The No Benefit to Bailee provision states that the policy will not benefit, either directly or indirectly, any bailee (a person who assumes custody of the property of others for business purposes).

G. The Other Sources of Recovery provision allows a PAP insurer to pay only the proportion that its limit of liability bears to the total applicable limits if other insurance coverage is available.

  1. Any physical damage coverage provided by the PAP for a nonowned auto is excess over any other collectible source of recovery.

  2. Other sources of recovery could include coverage provided by the owner of the nonowned auto, any other applicable physical damage insurance, and any other source of recovery that applies to the loss.

H. The Appraisal provision can be used if the insured and insurer disagree on the amount of loss.

 1. Either party may demand an appraisal of the loss.

 2. Each party selects a competent and impartial appraiser. The two appraisers then select an "umpire."

 3. If the appraisers cannot agree on the ACV and the amount of loss, any differences are submitted to the umpire. A decision by any two of the three is binding on all.

 4. Each party pays its chosen appraiser and shares equally the expenses of the appraisal and the umpire.

 5. If the insurer agrees to an appraisal, it does not waive any of its rights under the policy (that is, the policy conditions and exclusions would still apply).

Educational Objective 2

Given a case describing an auto physical damage claim, determine whether Part D—Coverage for Damage to Your Auto of the Personal Auto Policy would cover the claim and, if so, the amount the insurer would pay for the claim.

Key Points:

To adequately meet the requirements of this case study's educational objective, students should understand the DICE method of policy analysis, as well as the specific policy forms and endorsements described in the case, to make accurate coverage and loss settlement amount determinations.

To determine whether a policy covers a loss, many insurance professionals apply the DICE method. ("DICE" is an acronym for categories of policy provisions: declarations, insuring agreement, conditions, and exclusions.) The DICE method has four steps:

1. Review of the declarations page to determine whether it covers the person or the property at the time of the loss

2. Review of the insuring agreement to determine whether it covers the loss

3. Review of policy conditions to determine compliance

4. Review of policy exclusions to determine whether they preclude coverage of the loss

Each of these four steps is used in every case. Other categories of policy provisions should be examined. For example, endorsements and terms defined in the policy should be reviewed in relation to the declarations, insuring agreement, exclusions, and conditions.

Educational Objective 3

Describe the insured's duties following a covered auto accident or loss as shown in Part E of the Personal Auto Policy.

Key Points:

A person seeking coverage under the Personal Auto Policy (PAP) must perform the following general duties after an accident or a loss in order to receive payment under all of the policy's coverages:

A. General Duties

1. Provide prompt notice to the insurer—The insurer must be notified promptly of how, when, and where the accident or loss happened.

2. Cooperate with the insurer—The person seeking coverage must cooperate with the insurer in the investigation, settlement, or defense of any claim or suit related to the accident or loss.

3. Submit legal papers to the insurer—The person seeking coverage must promptly submit to the insurer copies of any notices or legal documentation received in connection with the accident or loss.

4. Submit to physical examination—The person seeking coverage must agree to submit to a physical examination conducted by a doctor chosen by the insurer upon request.

5. Agree to examination under oath—The person seeking coverage must agree to an examination under oath if required by the insurer.

6. Authorize release of medical records—The person seeking coverage must authorize the insurer to obtain medical reports and other pertinent records related to the claim.

7. Submit proof of loss—The person seeking coverage must submit a proof of loss when required by the insurer.

B. Additional Duties for Uninsured Motorists Coverage—A person seeking coverage under Part C—Uninsured Motorists Coverage must perform the following additional duties:

1. Notify police—The person seeking coverage must promptly notify police if a hit-and-run driver was involved in the accident.

2. Submit legal papers—If the person seeking coverage sues the uninsured motorist, the insured must submit to the insurer a copy of the legal documentation related to the suit.

C. Additional Duties for Physical Damage Coverage—The following additional duties are required under Part D—Coverage for Damage to Your Auto:

1. Prevent further loss—The person seeking coverage must take reasonable steps after a loss to protect a covered auto or non-owned auto and its equipment from further loss.

2. Notify police—If a covered auto or nonowned auto is stolen, the person seeking coverage must promptly notify police of the theft.

3. Permit inspection and appraisal—The person seeking coverage must permit the insurer to inspect and appraise the damaged property before its repair or disposal.

Educational Objective 4

Summarize each of the general provisions in Part F of the Personal Auto Policy.

Key Points:

Part F—General Provisions of the Personal Auto Policy (PAP) contains general provisions and conditions that apply to the entire policy.

A. Bankruptcy of Insured—If the insured declares bankruptcy or becomes insolvent, the insurer is not relieved of any obligations under the policy.

B. Changes in the Policy—Indicates that the policy contains all the agreements between the named insured and the insurer.

   1. The terms of the policy cannot be changed or waived except by an endorsement issued by the insurer.

   2. Changes during the policy term that can increase or decrease the premium include the following:

      a. The number, type, or use of insured vehicles

      b. The operators using insured vehicles

      c. The place of principal garaging of insured vehicles

      d. The coverage provided, deductibles, or limits of liability

   3. A liberalization clause automatically provides broadened coverage under some conditions.

C. Fraud—No coverage exists for any insured who makes fraudulent statements or engages in fraudulent conduct in connection with any accident or loss for which a claim is made.

D. Legal Action Against the Insurer—No legal action can be brought against the insurer until the insured has fully complied with all of the policy terms.

E. Insurer's Right to Recover Payment

   1. If the insurer makes a loss payment to a person who has the right to recover damages from a third party that either caused or is legally liable for the loss, the insurer has a legal right of subrogation against that third party.

   2. The covered person must do whatever is necessary to enable the insurer to exercise its subrogation rights. In addition, the person to whom the loss payment was made is not allowed to do anything after the loss that would prejudice or impede the insurer's right of subrogation.

   3. The subrogation provision does not apply to physical damage
   coverages in regard to any person who is using a covered auto
   with a reasonable belief that he or she is entitled to do so.

   4. If a person receives a loss payment from an insurer and also
   recovers damages from another party, that person is required to
   hold the proceeds of the second recovery in trust for the insurer
   and to reimburse the insurer to the extent of the insurer's loss
   payment.

F. Policy Period and Territory—The PAP applies only to accidents
   and losses that occur during the policy period shown on the Declarations page and within the policy territory. The policy territory
   includes the United States, U.S. territories and possessions, Puerto
   Rico, and Canada.

G. Termination—The PAP contains a provision that applies to policy
   termination by either the insured or insurer. The termination
   provision consists of the following four parts:

   1. Cancellation—The named insured normally can cancel any-
   time during the policy period under the following conditions:

   a. The insurer has sixty days to investigate and determine
   whether a new applicant meets the insurer's underwriting
   standards.

   b. If the cancellation is for nonpayment of premium, the
   insurer must give the named insured at least ten days'
   notice; in all other cases, at least twenty days' notice must
   be given.

   c. After the policy has been in force for sixty days, or if it is a
   renewal or continuation policy, the insurer can cancel the
   policy only for certain reasons.

   2. Nonrenewal—The conditions under which the insurer can
   nonrenew vary according to the length of the policy period, as
   follows:

   a. If the policy period is less than six months, the insurer has
   the right to nonrenew every six months, beginning six
   months after the policy's original effective date.

   b. If the policy period is six months or longer, but less than a
   year, the insurer has the right to nonrenew at the end of the
   policy period.

   c. If the policy period is one year or longer, the insurer has the
   right to nonrenew at each anniversary of the policy's original effective date.

3. Automatic termination—If the insurer offers to renew the policy but the named insured does not accept the offer, the policy automatically terminates at the end of the current policy period. Failure to pay the renewal premium means that the named insured has not accepted the insurer's offer to renew the policy.

4. Other termination provisions—The policy contains the following three additional termination provisions:

   a. The insurer may choose to deliver the cancellation notice rather than mail it.

   b. If the policy is canceled, the named insured may be entitled to a premium refund.

   c. The effective date of cancellation stated in the cancellation notice becomes the end of the policy period.

H. Transfer of Insured's Interest in the Policy—The named insured's rights and duties under the policy cannot be assigned to another party without the insurer's written consent. If the named insured dies, the coverage is automatically continued to the end of the policy period for both the surviving spouse and the legal representative of the deceased.

I. Two or More Auto Policies—If two or more auto policies issued to the named insured by the same insurer apply to the same accident, the insurer's maximum limit of liability is the highest applicable limit of liability under any one policy.

Educational Objective 5

Describe the Personal Auto Policy endorsements that are used to handle common auto loss exposures.

Key Points:

Insurance professionals should be aware that, while the Personal Auto Policy (PAP) provides extensive coverage, additions or modifications may be necessary in some scenarios.

A. Miscellaneous Type Vehicle Endorsement

   1. The unmodified PAP excludes coverage for vehicles that have fewer than four wheels and vehicles designed for off-public-road use.

   2. This endorsement provides coverage for a motor home, a motorcycle or similar type of vehicle, an all-terrain vehicle, a dune buggy, or a golf cart, none of which are included in the PAP's definition of covered auto.

   3. The endorsement schedule lists each covered vehicle and the corresponding applicable coverages, limits of liability, and premiums.

   4. An optional passenger hazard exclusion, which excludes liability coverage for bodily injury to any person occupying the covered vehicle, can be activated as part of the endorsement.

   5. Part D (physical damage) of the endorsement excludes coverage for loss to clothing or luggage, business or office equipment, sales samples, or articles used in exhibits. It also limits the amount paid for physical damage losses to the lowest of these values:

      a. The stated amount shown in the schedule or declarations

      b. The actual cash value of the stolen or damaged property

      c. The amount necessary to repair or replace the property (less any deductible)

B. Snowmobile Endorsement

   1. A snowmobile is defined as a land motor vehicle propelled solely by wheels, crawler-type treads, belts, or similar mechanical devices and designed for use mainly off public roads on snow or ice.

   2. Available snowmobile coverages include liability, medical payments, uninsured motorists, collision, and other than collision.

   3. Each covered snowmobile is listed in a schedule that states the applicable coverages, limits of liability, and premiums.

4. The liability coverage for snowmobiles has several exclusions and modifications:

   a. Coverage does not apply if the snowmobile is used in any business.

   b. Coverage does not apply when the snowmobile is used in a race or speed contest or in practice or preparation for a race, regardless of whether the race is prearranged or organized.

   c. Coverage is excluded for any person or organization, other than the named insured, while renting or leasing a snowmobile.

   d. A passenger hazard exclusion can be activated that excludes liability for bodily injury to any person while occupying or being towed by the snowmobile.

C. Trailer/Camper Body Coverage (Maximum Limit of Liability)

   1. Coverage is extended to direct and accidental loss to a trailer or camper body described in the policy declarations or the schedule of the endorsement.

   2. The endorsement also provides coverage for related facilities or equipment, including, but not limited to, cooking, dining, plumbing, or refrigeration facilities, as well as awnings or cabanas.

   3. Loss to clothing or luggage, business or office equipment, and sales samples or articles used in exhibitions is excluded.

D. Extended Non-Owned Coverage—Vehicles Furnished or Available for Regular Use

   1. The unendorsed PAP excludes liability and medical payments coverage for vehicles furnished or made available for the regular use of the named insured and family members. This exclusion can be eliminated by adding this endorsement.

   2. The endorsement's coverage applies only to the individual(s) named in the endorsement schedule. However, coverage can be extended to the named individual's family members.

   3. The liability coverage provided by the endorsement is excess over any other applicable insurance on the nonowned vehicle.

   4. The endorsement schedule indicates separate premiums for liability and for medical payments coverage.

E. Named Non-Owner Coverage

   1. People who do not regularly own an auto or who occasionally drive another person's vehicle or a rental vehicle can secure coverage for the loss exposures arising out of their use of a nonowned auto with this endorsement.

2. This endorsement provides liability coverage, medical payments coverage, uninsured motorists coverage, and underinsured motorists (but not physical damage) coverage.

3. This coverage applies only to a person who is actually named in the endorsement. Coverage for family members can be included by indicating such coverage on the endorsement schedule.

4. The liability insurance under a PAP with the named nonowner endorsement is excess over any other applicable liability insurance on the nonowned auto.

5. The endorsement provides the named insured with liability, medical payments, uninsured motorists, and underinsured motorists coverage on a newly acquired vehicle for up to fourteen days.

F. Auto Loan/Lease Coverage

1. This endorsement amends the Part D (physical damage) coverage of the PAP so that, in the event of the loss, coverage is included for the unpaid amount due on the lease or loan.

2. The endorsement provides coverage for the difference between the outstanding loan amount and the amount that would have been paid based on the limit of liability as stated in the unendorsed policy (actual cash value or the amount necessary to repair or replace the property with like kind and quality).

3. None of these would be included in any loss payment:
   a. Lease or loan payments that were overdue at the time of loss
   b. Penalties imposed under a lease for excessive use, abnormal wear and tear, or high mileage
   c. Security deposits not refunded by a lessor
   d. Costs for extended warranties; credit life insurance; or health, accident, or disability insurance purchased with the loan or the lease
   e. Balances transferred from previous loans or leases

G. Limited Mexico Coverage

1. The unendorsed PAP does not provide any coverage in Mexico.

2. This endorsement extends the PAP coverages to an insured who is involved in an accident or loss in Mexico within twenty-five miles of the United States border on a trip of ten days or less.

3. The endorsement is effective only if primary liability coverage is also purchased from a licensed Mexican insurer. Mexican insurance usually can be purchased from a licensed agent at the border.

4. The liability insurance provided by the endorsement is excess over the Mexican insurance.

5. The major advantage of the endorsement is that it provides additional liability insurance beyond that provided by the Mexican policy, as well as providing the other standard PAP coverages, such as physical damage coverage.

H. Excess Electronic Equipment Coverage

1. The unendorsed PAP excludes coverage for loss to any electronic equipment that is not permanently installed in the insured vehicle and also excludes coverage for loss to tapes, records, disks, or other media.

2. The PAP also includes a $1,000 limit on electronic equipment that reproduces, receives, or transmits audio, visual, or data signals that are permanently installed in locations not intended for that purpose by the auto manufacturer.

3. The endorsement can be used to increase the limit on such equipment from $1,000 to a limit shown in the endorsement schedule.

4. The endorsement also provides coverage for direct and accidental loss to tapes, records, disks, or other media owned by the named insured or the named insured's family member.

   a. Coverage is provided for the lesser of the actual cash value or the amount necessary to repair or replace the stolen or damaged property, subject to a maximum limit of $200 for all such media.

   b. The media must be in or upon the covered auto or any nonowned auto at the time of loss.

I. Coverage for Damage to Your Auto (Maximum Limit of Liability)

1. This endorsement allows owners of high-value antique cars or restored show cars to establish the car's insurable value when the policy is written by inserting a stated amount of insurance in the policy.

2. Each vehicle is described and a stated amount of insurance is shown that applies to collision loss and other than collision loss.

3. The insurer's maximum limit of liability for a covered loss is limited to the lowest of these values:

   a. The stated amount shown in the schedule or in the declarations

    b. The actual cash value of the stolen or damaged property

    c. The amount necessary to repair or replace the property with other property of like kind and quality

  4. This endorsement states that if a repair or replacement of the vehicle results in better than like kind or quality, the insurer will not include the amount of betterment in any loss payment.

J. Optional Limits Transportation Expenses Coverage

  1. The PAP provides coverage up to a limit of $20 per day for temporary transportation expenses.

  2. This endorsement allows the insured to increase coverage to one of three limits, which can be applied to the costs of a substitute vehicle for the period reasonably required to repair or replace the auto.

K. Towing and Labor Costs Coverage

  1. This endorsement provides coverage for the costs of towing the covered auto when it is disabled. The cost of labor performed to repair the auto at the place of disablement is also covered up to the limit.

  2. A single limit per disablement applies whether it is used for towing or labor costs. A separate limit applies to each disablement.

Educational Objective 6

Given a case describing an auto claim, determine whether the Personal Auto Policy would cover the claim and, if so, the amount the insurer would pay for the claim.

Key Points:

To adequately meet the requirements of this case study's educational objective, students should understand the DICE method of policy analysis, as well as the specific policy forms and endorsements described in the case, to make accurate coverage and loss settlement amount determinations.

Apply the steps in the DICE method to the specific issues of the coverage claim.

To determine whether a policy covers a loss, many insurance professionals apply the DICE method. ("DICE" is an acronym for categories of policy provisions: declarations, insuring agreement, conditions, and exclusions.) The DICE method has four steps:

1. Review of the declarations page to determine whether it covers the person or the property at the time of the loss
2. Review of the insuring agreement to determine whether it covers the loss
3. Review of policy conditions to determine compliance
4. Review of policy exclusions to determine whether they preclude coverage of the loss

Each of these four steps is used in every case. Other categories of policy provisions should be examined. For example, endorsements and terms defined in the policy should be reviewed in relation to the declarations, insuring agreement, exclusions, and conditions.

Key Words and Phrases:

Key Words

Physical damage coverages
There are four kinds: comprehensive—pays for loss to covered auto or its equipment from any cause not excluded, except collision or overturn; specified causes of loss—provides named peril coverage; collision—covers loss to a covered auto or its equipment by collision with another object or by overturn; and towing—provides coverage for towing and labor performed at the place of disablement.

Deductible
A portion of a covered loss that is not paid by the insurer.

Transportation expenses
Coverage extension for substitute transportation costs incurred when a private passenger type auto has been stolen.

Actual cash value (ACV)
Cost to replace property with new property of like kind and quality less depreciation.

Appraisal
A method of resolving disputes between insurers and insureds over the amount owed on a covered loss.

Proof of loss
A statement of facts about a loss for which the insured is making a claim.

Liberalization clause
A policy condition providing that if a policy form is broadened at no additional premium, the broadened coverage automatically applies to all existing policies of the same type.

Policy termination
The ending of the contractual relationship between the insured and insurer by cancellation, expiration, or nonrenewal.

Cancellation
Termination of a policy, by either the insurer or the insured, during the policy term.

Homeowners Property Coverage

5

Educational Objective 1

Describe how individuals and families can use the ISO Homeowners insurance program to address their personal risk management needs.

Key Points:

The Insurance Services Office (ISO) Homeowners (HO) program provides six policy forms designed to meet the various risk management needs of individuals and families.

A. ISO Homeowners Program

All of the ISO HO forms provide property coverage designed for the needs of specific types of insurance buyers. In addition to property coverage, each form also provides loss of use, personal liability, and medical payments coverages.

1. The HO-2—Broad Form (HO 00 02) provides named perils coverage for dwellings, other structures, and personal property.

2. The HO-3—Special Form (HO 00 03) provides special form coverage on dwellings and other structures (rather than the named perils coverage provided by the HO-2).

3. The HO-4—Contents Broad Form (HO 00 04) provides coverage for a tenant's personal property on a named perils basis. It does not cover dwellings or other structures.

4. The HO-5—Comprehensive Form (HO 00 05) provides open perils coverage on dwellings, other structures, and personal property. It provides the broadest coverage available among ISO's forms for property.

5. The HO-6—Unit-Owners Form (HO 00 06) provides coverage for personal property on a named perils basis, with limited dwelling coverage (unit improvements and betterments). The HO-6 is designed to meet the risk management needs of the owners of condominium units and cooperative apartment shares.

Study Tips

Read actively, and use the review questions to reinforce your learning.

6. The HO-8—Modified Coverage Form (HO 00 08) provides coverage for a dwelling, other structures, and personal property, on a limited, named perils basis.

   a. A special valuation clause specifies that damage will be covered on a functional replacement cost basis.

   b. The HO-8 is designed to meet the risk management needs of owners-occupants of dwellings who may not meet insurer underwriting standards required for other policy forms (such as when the replacement cost of a dwelling significantly exceeds the dwelling's market value).

Educational Objective 2

Summarize the factors and adjustments important to rating homeowners insurance.

Key Points:

Insurers charge a premium for the various homeowners insurance policies they offer that is based on homeowners rating factors and adjustments. To develop rating factors and adjustments, insurers typically use a framework designed by ISO that includes the development of a base premium, base premium adjustments, and final adjustments.

A. Base Premium Factors

The base premium is influenced by several factors, including these:

1. Dwelling location—a geographical division within a state
2. Public protection class—a ranking of the fire protection (including available water and water pressure) provided in the area
3. Construction factors—two broad classifications (frame and masonry) of construction, along with other construction factors
4. Coverage amount—The coverage amount required for a dwelling
5. Policy form—The policy form selected, depending on how broad the coverage is

B. Base Premium Adjustments

The base premium is adjusted to reflect variations in risk management requirements and loss exposures. Base premium adjustments can include these:

1. Endorsements—Some endorsements provide credits or charges that affect the premium.
2. Unusual construction type—Dwellings with construction that varies from the basic frame and masonry classifications may receive a rate adjustment.
3. Deductible changes—The standard deductible for all ISO policies is $250. The deductible can be increased in increments up to $2,500 for a premium credit or decreased to $100 for a premium charge.

C. Final Adjustments

The insurer develops the final premium by applying final adjustments such as these, which can vary from state to state:

1. Claim history

2. Insurance score—In some states, insurers apply an insurance score, a numerical ranking based on many of the factors that comprise an individual's credit history.

3. Package policy credits—Some insurers offer package policy credits, or policy discounts, to customers who place more than one line of business with them. These credits reflect the economies realized by the insurer from servicing more than one policy for the same policyholder.

Educational Objective 3
Describe the structure of the Homeowners policy (HO-3).

Key Points:

The HO-3 policy provides property and liability coverages for owner-occupants of a one- to four-family dwellings. The HO-3 policy consists of primary components.

A. Declarations page provides answers to questions:
  1. Who is the policyholder?
  2. Where is the policyholder's residence?
  3. What are the coverage limits?
  4. What is the premium?
  5. What is the Section I deductible?
  6. What is the effective date of the policy?
  7. What forms and endorsements apply to the policy?
  8. Who is the mortgage holder?

B. Agreement and Definitions
  1. The Agreement (also known as the insuring agreement) establishes the basis for the contract and specifies what the insurer and policyholder will do for each other. The insurer agrees to provide coverage, and the policyholder agrees to pay the premium and comply with the policy conditions.
  2. Definitions provide special meanings that some words or phrases have when they are used within the policy. These words or phrases appear in the policy within quotation marks.

C. Section I—Property Coverages specifies the property covered, the perils for which the property is covered, and the exclusions and conditions that affect property coverages and losses.
  1. Coverage A—Dwelling (divided into five property coverages) applies to the dwelling on the "residence premises" listed on the Declarations page. It also applies to structures attached to the dwelling.
  2. Coverage B—Other Structures applies to structures on the residence premises, other than the dwelling building, that are not attached to the dwelling.
  3. Coverage C—Personal Property applies to the contents of the insured property and to the insured's personal property anywhere in the world.

4. Coverage D—Loss of Use applies to the insured's exposure to financial loss, apart from the property damage itself, if the residence premises where the insured resides are damaged so badly that they are unfit for residence.

5. Additional Coverages applies to additional coverages provided, subject to certain limitations.

D. Section II—Liability Coverages is divided into two coverages:

1. Coverage E—Personal Liability applies to third-party coverage for those who are injured or whose property is damaged by an insured.

2. Coverage F—Medical payments to Others covers the necessary medical expenses incurred by others (not an insured) within three years of an injury.

E. Endorsements can increase or decrease limits of an HO-3 policy, add or remove coverages, change definitions, clarify policy intent, or recognize specific characteristics that require a premium increase or decrease.

Educational Objective 4

Summarize each of the HO-3 policy provisions in the following Section I—Property Coverages:

- **Coverage A—Dwelling**

- **Coverage B—Other Structures**

- **Coverage C—Personal Property**

- **Coverage D—Loss of Use**

- **Additional Coverages**

Key Points:

The HO-3 Section I—Property Coverages of the Homeowners 3—
Special Form (HO-3) provides coverages for a house and its contents.
It is divided into five property coverages.

A. Coverage A—Dwelling applies to the dwelling on the "residence
premises" listed on the Declarations page. The Coverage A limit
is based on the cost to replace the dwelling; the cost of the land
should not be included.

   1. Coverage A also applies to these types of property:

   a. Structures attached to the dwelling—such as a garage
   or deck

   b. Materials and supplies that are located on or next to the
   covered dwelling that are used to construct or repair the
   dwelling

   2. The land at the residence premises is specifically excluded from
   property coverage.

B. Coverage B—Other Structures applies to other structures on the
residence premises that are not attached to the dwelling and are
separated from the dwelling by "clear space."

   1. Coverage B has a limit that is 10 percent of the limit for
   Coverage A—Dwelling. It applies collectively to all "other
   structures" at the residence premises.

   2. Coverage B excludes coverage of buildings meeting any of
   these criteria:

   a. A structure rented to anyone not a resident (unless rented
   as a private garage)

   b. A structure from which any business is conducted

   c. A structure used to store business property

C. Coverage C—Personal Property

   1. Coverage C covers these types of property:

     a. An insured's personal property not only in the insured's residence, but anywhere in the world

     b. Personal property owned by others while in the residence premises, if the insured requests such coverage after a loss

     c. Personal property owned by a guest or residence employee while the property is in any residence occupied by the insured

   2. The Coverage C standard limit is 50 percent of the Coverage A limit.

     a. Only 10 percent of the Coverage C limit, or $1,000 (whichever is greater), is provided for property usually located at a residence other than the residence listed on the Declarations page.

     b. The 10 percent limitation does not apply to personal property that is moved from the residence premises because the house is being repaired, renovated, or rebuilt and is not fit to live or store property in.

     c. An insured who is moving from one principal residence to another will have the full limit of Coverage C (without the 10 percent limit) available at both locations for thirty days.

     d. Special sublimits—Some categories of personal property that have high values or may be targets to theft are subject to smaller sublimits, such as $200 on money and precious metals and $2,500 for property on residence premises used primarily for any business purpose.

   3. Property not covered—personal property usually insured through policies other than the homeowners policy.

D. Coverage D—Loss of Use applies to the insured's exposure to financial loss, apart from the property damage itself, if the residence premises are damaged so badly that they are not fit to live in.

   1. Coverage D is provided at a limit that is 30 percent of the Coverage A limit and applies in addition to the Coverage A limit. The Coverage D limit can be increased, for an additional premium, by changing the amount appearing on the Declarations page.

   2. Three coverages are grouped under Coverage D:

     a. Additional living expense—if the insured individual or family must live elsewhere until their dwelling has been repaired

     b. Fair rental value—if part of the residence is rented to others and a covered loss makes that part not fit to live in

    c. Loss of use due to civil authority—if civil authorities prohibit property owners from using their residence premises because neighboring property is damaged

E. Additional Coverages—Twelve additional coverages are included in the HO-3, subject to certain limitations.

    1. Debris removal—If the amount to be paid for the actual damage to the property plus the debris removal expense is more than the limit of liability for the damaged property, an additional 5 percent of the limit is available for debris removal.

    2. Reasonable repairs—Covers reasonable cost of the measures taken to protect the property from further damage.

    3. Trees, shrubs, and other plants—Up to 5 percent of Coverage A, with a maximum of $500 for any one tree, plant, or shrub.

    4. Fire department service charge—Up to $500.

    5. Property removed—When property is removed from a home that is endangered by a covered peril, it is covered for up to thirty days.

    6. Credit card, electronic fund transfer card or access device, forgery, and counterfeit money—Up to $500 for legal obligations.

    7. Loss assessment—Up to $1,000 for the insured's share.

    8. Collapse—Covered when it results from covered perils, but not from defective materials or methods of construction.

    9. Glass or safety glazing material—Coverage is excluded if the dwelling has been vacant for more than sixty days before the loss.

    10. Landlord's furnishings—Covered up to $2,500. Theft is excluded.

    11. Ordinance or law—Coverage of up to 10 percent of the Coverage A limit is provided for the increased cost incurred due to the enforcement of any law or ordinance.

    12. Grave markers—Grave markers and mausoleums are covered up to $5,000.

Educational Objective 5
Summarize each of the HO-3 policy provisions in Section I—Perils Insured Against.

Key Points:

The HO-3 policy protects policyholders' homes, buildings, and personal property against loss from a variety of perils.

A. Insured perils for Coverage A—Dwelling and Coverage B—Other Structures are grouped together because both coverages provide special form coverage for real property items with similar exposures to loss.

1. Section I—Exclusions apply to all coverages in Section I, including Coverages A and B:

   a. Collapse

   b. Freezing of a plumbing, heating, air conditioning, or sprinkler system, or a household appliance

   c. Freezing, thawing, pressure, or weight of water or ice

   d. Theft of construction materials

   e. Vandalism and malicious mischief to vacant dwellings

   f. Mold, fungus, or wet rot

   g. Natural deterioration

   h. Smoke from agricultural smudging or industrial operations

   i. Pollutants

   j. Settling of the dwelling

   k. Animals

2. Exceptions to excluded perils

   a. Water damage coverage—Unless the loss is otherwise excluded, the HO-3 covers water damage to buildings or other structures that results from an accidental discharge or overflow of water or steam. The water or steam must come from a plumbing, heating, air conditioning, or sprinkler system; from a household appliance on the residence premises; or from a storm drain or water, steam, or sewer pipe off the residence premises.

   b. Ensuing losses—Ensuing losses not specifically excluded by the HO-3 are covered.

B. Coverage C—Personal Property applies to the contents of a home and other personal property on a named perils basis.

    1. Because Coverage C lists the named perils for which coverage is provided, coverage for personal property under the HO-3 is not as broad as the special form coverage for dwellings and other structures.

    2. Coverage C applies to these named perils:

        a. Fire or lightning

        b. Windstorm or hail

        c. Explosion

        d. Riot or civil commotion

        e. Aircraft

        f. Vehicles

        g. Smoke

        h. Vandalism or malicious mischief

        i. Theft

        j. Falling objects

        k. Weight of ice, snow, or sleet

        l. Accidental discharge or overflow of water or steam

        m. Sudden and accidental tearing apart, cracking, burning, or bulging

        n. Freezing

        o. Sudden and accidental damage from artificially generated electrical current

        p. Volcanic eruption

Educational Objective 6

Summarize each of the HO-3 policy provisions in Section I—Exclusions.

Key Points:

Any loss to a dwelling or other structure or consequential loss of use under a Homeowners 3 (HO-3) policy and special form (open perils) coverage is covered unless the cause of loss is specifically excluded. Section I personal property coverages are on a named peril basis (subject to exclusions).

A. Section I—Exclusions preclude coverage for damage to or loss of buildings and personal property caused by some perils. These are the Section I exclusions:

1. Ordinance or Law—Excludes coverage for losses resulting from any ordinance or law that reduces the value of property; that requires testing for or clean up of pollutants; or that requires demolition, construction, or debris removal.

2. Earth Movement—Excludes coverage for losses resulting from earthquake and other types of earth movement, such as landslides, mudslides, mudflows, mine subsidence, and sinkholes.

3. Water Damage—Excludes coverage for losses caused by flood, surface water, waves, and water or water-borne material such as sewage that backs up through sewers and drains. However, ensuing losses from fire, explosion, or theft resulting from water damage are covered.

4. Power Failure—Excludes coverage for damage resulting from a loss of electrical power or utility service because of a problem away from the insured premises. However, if power is interrupted by an insured peril that occurs on the premises, resulting losses are covered.

5. Neglect—Excludes coverage for losses resulting from an insured's failure to use all reasonable means to protect property at the time of a loss and after a loss occurs. The insurer agrees to pay the cost of reasonable repairs to protect damaged property under an additional coverage.

6. War—Excludes coverage for property losses that result from war, including the discharge of nuclear weapons. This exclusion applies to undeclared war, civil war, insurrection, rebellion, or revolution.

7. Nuclear Hazard—Excludes coverage for property losses that occur because of a nuclear hazard, defined in Section I—Conditions as any nuclear reaction, radiation, or contamination.

8. Intentional Loss—Excludes coverage for any loss arising out of any act that any insured commits or conspires to commit with the intent to cause a loss. The exclusion applies to all insureds, even if only one commits an act with intent.

9. Governmental Action—Excludes coverage for losses resulting from the destruction, confiscation, or seizure by order of any governmental or public authority. This exclusion does not preclude coverage for governmental action taken to prevent the spread of fire.

B. Section I—Exclusions contains an additional three exclusions (weather conditions, act or decisions, and faulty workmanship) that apply only to Coverage A—Dwelling and Coverage B—Other Structures.

1. These exclusions are sometimes called the concurrent causation exclusions, because other causes of loss or perils, such as fire or water damage, often follow or "ensue," or are concurrent, with any one of the three excluded causes of loss.

   a. Concurrent causation involves loss from two or more perils occurring either at the same time or in sequence. Such losses may not only involve ensuing type losses, but may also be triggered by such perils as flood, earthquake, war, or nuclear reaction.

   b. The HO-3 policy excludes coverage for losses directly resulting from these perils, but any ensuing loss is covered unless precluded elsewhere in the policy.

2. The three exclusions that apply only to Coverages A and B are these:

   a. Weather conditions—Excludes coverage for losses resulting from weather conditions only if a weather condition contributes to any of the previously excluded perils.

   b. Acts or decisions—Excludes coverage for losses resulting from acts or decisions, including the failure to act or decide, of any person, group, organization or government body.

   c. Faulty workmanship—Excludes coverage for damage that results from faulty construction, planning, or materials, including faulty zoning, surveying, design specifications, workmanship, construction, renovation, and maintenance.

Educational Objective 7

Summarize each of the HO-3 policy provisions in Section I—Conditions.

Key Points:

Eighteen major conditions apply to the Section I coverages in the HO-3 policy. Both the insured and the insurer must meet these conditions.

A. Insurable Interest and Limit of Liability—The maximum payment for any single loss is the applicable limit shown on the Declarations page, regardless of the number of insureds who have an insurable interest in the property. This condition further limits loss payment to any insured to the extent of that insured's insurable interest in the property at the time of the loss.

B. Your Duties After Loss—The insured has these duties:
  1. Give prompt notice after a loss has occurred
  2. Notify the police if the loss is by theft
  3. Notify the credit card, electronic fund transfer card company, or access device company
  4. Protect the property from further damage
  5. Cooperate with the insurer during the investigation
  6. Prepare an inventory of the damaged personal property
  7. Verify the loss, which may include furnishing records and submitting to an examination under oath
  8. Sign a sworn proof of loss

C. Loss Settlement—This condition establishes two methods for determining the amount to be paid for a property loss:
  1. Losses under Coverage C—Personal Property and for miscellaneous items are settled for the lesser of two amounts:
    a. Actual cash value (ACV) at the time of the loss
    b. The amount required to repair or replace the items
  2. Losses under Coverage A—Dwelling and Coverage B—Other Structures depend on how the limit of insurance compares to the replacement cost value of the damaged buildings at the time of the loss.
    a. If the limit of insurance is 80 percent or more of the replacement cost, the insurer will pay for the replacement cost of the damage up to the limit of coverage.

b. If the limit of insurance is less than 80 percent of the replacement cost, the insurer will pay the greater of the ACV of the damage or the proportion of the cost to repair or replace the damage that the limit of insurance bears to 80 percent of the replacement cost.

D. Loss to a Pair or Set—This condition establishes the amount the insurer is willing to pay if an item that is part of a pair or set is damaged or lost.

E. Appraisal—This condition outlines a method for resolving the disagreement if the insured and the insurer cannot agree on the amount of a loss.

1. The insured and the insurer both choose an appraiser. If their estimates differ, they submit them to an umpire.

2. An agreement of any two of those three can set the amount of the loss.

F. Other Insurance and Service Agreement—This condition explains how losses will be settled:

1. If two or more insurance policies cover the same loss, they share the loss proportionately.

2. If personal property is covered by a service agreement, homeowners insurance coverage applies in excess over any amounts payable under the service agreement.

G. Suit Against Us—An insured is barred from bringing legal action against the insurer unless the insured has complied with all policy provisions. Any legal action must be started within two years of the loss.

H. Our Option—Whether to repair or replace damaged property is the insurer's option.

I. Loss Payment—Generally, a loss is payable sixty days after the insurer receives a proof of loss and either the insurer and the insured have reached an agreement or a court judgment or appraisal award has been entered.

J. Abandonment of Property—If the insured abandons the property after it is damaged or destroyed, the insurer need not take responsibility for it.

K. Mortgage Clause—The mortgagee listed on the Declarations page has these rights:

1. A loss to property covered by Coverages A or B is payable jointly to the mortgagee and the insured.

2. The mortgagee retains the right to collect from the insurer its insurable interest in the property.

3. An insurer must mail notice of policy cancellation or nonrenewal to the mortgagee (in addition to the insured) at least ten days before the cancellation or nonrenewal.

L. No Benefit to Bailee—A bailee who holds the property of an insured is responsible for the care of that property.

M. Nuclear Hazard Clause—This condition defines the nuclear hazard for which coverage is excluded in Section I—Exclusions.

N. Recovered Property—If the insurer pays a claim for the loss of property, and the property is later recovered, the insured has the option of taking the property and returning the claim payment and allowing the insurer to take over the property.

O. Volcanic Eruption Period—All volcanic eruptions that occur within a seventy-two hour period are considered to be one volcanic eruption.

P. Policy Period—Coverage applies only to losses that occur during the policy period.

Q. Concealment or Fraud—Any insured who conceals or misrepresents any material information, engages in fraudulent conduct, or makes false statements relating to the insurance is not covered under the policy.

R. Loss Payable Clause—The insurer agrees to include the named loss payee when a claim is paid involving that personal property. The loss payee is also entitled to notification if the policy is canceled or nonrenewed.

Educational Objective 8

Given a case describing a homeowners property claim, determine whether the HO-3 Policy Section I—Property Coverages would cover the claim and, if so, the amount the insurer would pay for the claim.

Key Points:

To adequately meet the requirements of this case study's educational objective, students should understand the DICE method of policy analysis as well as the specific policy forms and endorsements described in the case to make accurate coverage and loss settlement amount determinations.

To determine whether a policy covers a loss, many insurance professionals apply the DICE method. ("DICE" is an acronym for categories of policy provisions: declarations, insuring agreement, conditions, and exclusions.) The DICE method has four steps:

1. Review of the declarations page to determine whether it covers the person or the property at the time of the loss
2. Review of the insuring agreement to determine whether it covers the loss
3. Review of policy conditions to determine compliance
4. Review of policy exclusions to determine whether they preclude coverage of the loss

Each of these four steps is used in every case. Other categories of policy provisions should be examined. For example, endorsements and terms defined in the policy should be reviewed in relation to the declarations, insuring agreement, exclusions, and conditions.

Key Words and Phrases:

Key Words

Named perils coverage
An insurance policy where the covered causes of loss are listed or "named" in the policy.

Special form coverage
Property insurance coverage covering all causes of loss not specifically excluded.

Functional replacement cost
The cost of replacing damaged property with similar property that performs the same function but might not be identical to the damaged property.

Building Code Effectiveness Grading Schedule (BCEGS)
A rating classification based on the quality of a community's building codes and the level of their enforcement; ranges from 1 to 10.

Named peril
A specific cause of loss listed and described in an insurance policy. Also used to describe policies containing named perils.

Inherent vice
A quality of or condition within a particular type of property that tends to make the property destroy itself.

Ensuing loss
The loss attributable to a subsequent peril that results from loss by an initial peril.

Concurrent causation (concurrent causation doctrine)
A legal doctrine stating that if a loss can be attributed to two or more independent concurrent causes—one or more excluded by the policy and one covered—then the policy covers the loss.

Insurable interest
An interest in the subject of an insurance policy that is not unduly remote and that would cause the interested party to suffer financial loss if an insured event occurred.

Homeowners Liability Coverage

6

Key Points:

The Section II—Liability Coverages provided by Insurance Services Office's (ISO's) HO-3 form addresses the third-party liability exposures of individuals and families resulting from owning and using property and their personal activities.

A. Coverage E—Personal Liability Coverage provides coverage if a claim is made against an insured because of bodily injury or property damage arising from a covered occurrence.

   1. This coverage, which applies worldwide, applies to bodily injury and property damage arising from the insured's activities or premises. In most instances, such liability arises from the insured's negligence.

   2. Basic personal liability limits are $100,000 per occurrence, with higher limits available for an additional premium.

   3. Defense costs coverage is provided even if a suit is groundless, false, or fraudulent.

   4. The insurer's obligation to defend ends only when the liability limit for the occurrence is exhausted by payment of a settlement or judgment (even if policy limits are exhausted by the costs of the claim).

B. Coverage F—Medical Payments to Others covers medical payments incurred by others (not an insured or regular household residents) within three years of an injury.

   1. Eligible medical expenses include reasonable charges for medical, surgical, x-ray, dental, ambulance, hospital, professional nursing, and funeral services, and prosthetic devices.

Study Tips

After you complete the last assignment in the Review Notes, you should be ready for the exam. For complete information regarding exam dates and fees, visit our Web page, www.TheInstitutes.org/forms, where you can access and print exam registration information.

2. Medical Payments to Others coverage is automatically included in all homeowners policies for a limit generally set at $1,000 per person for a single accident. This limit can be increased for an additional premium.

3. Medical Payments to Others coverage is sometimes considered to overlap with bodily injury liability coverage. However, liability coverage applies only when an insured is legally responsible for damages.

4. Claims for medical payments are often paid when the insured feels a moral obligation to another person, even though the insured is not negligent or legally responsible.

5. When a bodily injury claim involves a relatively small amount of money, paying it as a Medical Payments to Others claim simplifies matters by eliminating any need to determine whether an insured was legally responsible for the injuries.

6. Coverage F—Medical Payments to Others coverage applies under these conditions:

    a. The injury occurs to a person who has the insured's permission to be at the insured's location.

    b. The injured person is away from the insured location, and bodily injury arises out of a condition at the insured location or on property immediately adjoining the insured's location.

    c. A person is injured while away from the insured location by an activity performed by an insured.

    d. A person is injured away from the insured location by an insured's residence employee who, while off the insured premises and in the course of his or her employment for the insured, causes bodily injury.

    e. An individual is injured by an animal owned by or in the care of an insured while off the insured premises.

C. The Section II—Additional Coverages provision supplements the protection provided by Coverages E and F. Section II—Additional Coverages include four additional coverages:

    1. The Claim Expense additional coverage will pay these expenses:

        a. Expenses we incur—These include the insurer's expenses to provide the insured's legal representation when a claim occurs.

        b. Premiums on bonds—If any bonds are required in the defense of a suit, the insurer pays the bond premiums.

c. Reasonable expenses—If an insurer requests an insured's assistance in the investigation or defense of a claim or suit, the insurer pays for any reasonable expenses incurred by the insured, including loss of earnings, parking costs, meals, and mileage.

d. Postjudgment interest—Such interest can be incurred after a judgment has been made against an insured. The interest is accrued on the amount owed to a plaintiff until the insurer makes the payment.

2. The First Aid Expenses additional coverage states that an insurer will reimburse an insured for expenses incurred when rendering first aid to others as a result of bodily injury.

3. The Damage to Property of Others additional coverage, sometimes called "voluntary property damage" coverage, pays up to $1,000 for damage to property of others caused by an insured, regardless of fault or legal liability.

a. This coverage allows an insured to maintain goodwill by paying for relatively minor losses to another person's property, and it allows the insurer to avoid litigation expenses on small property damage claims.

b. An insurer will not pay under this additional coverage for property damage to the extent of any amount recoverable under Section I of the policy.

c. The insurer will not pay for property damage in several different circumstances, such as damage caused intentionally by the insured or damage to property owned by the insured.

4. Loss Assessment additional coverage applies to homeowners that are billed with an assessment by their homeowners associations or similar organizations when the organization sustains a loss for which its officers failed to secure a sufficient amount of insurance.

a. The coverage provides up to $1,000 for an insured's share of a loss assessment.

b. The coverage applies when the loss involves bodily injury or property damage that is not excluded under Section II of the homeowners policy or when liability results from an act of an elected and unpaid director, officer, or trustee.

Educational Objective 2

Summarize each of the HO-3 policy provisions in Section II—Exclusions.

Key Points:

Twenty-two exclusions limit the scope of the personal liability coverage in the HO-3 policy. The first twelve exclusions apply to both Coverages E and F. Of the remaining exclusions, six apply only to Coverage E and four apply only to Coverage F.

A. The first four of the twelve exclusions that apply to both Coverages E and F are a detailed set of exclusions for losses arising out of motor vehicles, watercraft, aircraft, and hovercraft.

   1. Motor Vehicle Liability exclusion—Limits the majority of personal motor vehicle loss exposures that would typically be insured under a Personal Auto Policy (PAP).

   a. The homeowners policy defines a motor vehicle as any self-propelled vehicle, including an attached trailer.

   b. The exclusion applies to a motor vehicle that meets any of these criteria:
   - It is required by law to be registered for use on public roads or property.
   - It is involved in an organized race.
   - It is rented to others.
   - It is used to carry persons or cargo for a charge.
   - It is used for any business purpose, except for motorized golf carts used on a golf course.

   c. The homeowners policy provides some coverages for certain motor vehicles specifically related to personal, residential use.

   2. Watercraft Liability exclusion—Similar to the motor vehicle exclusion. However, it does not apply to small, low-powered watercraft or watercraft the insured uses but does not own.

   3. Aircraft Liability exclusion—Precludes coverage for all aircraft. However, because model airplanes or hobby aircraft do not carry people or cargo, they are covered.

   4. Hovercraft Liability exclusion—Hovercraft are excluded with no exceptions. Hovercraft are self-propelled motorized ground effect air cushion vehicles.

B. Coverage E—Personal Liability and Coverage F—Medical Payments to Others contain eight additional exclusions that apply to both of these coverages:

1. Expected or Intended Injury—Excludes coverage for losses caused by an insured when the bodily injury or property damage is intentional or expected, even if the actual injury or damage resulting from the action was unintended when the intentional action took place.

2. Business—Excludes coverage for bodily injury or property damage claims arising out of a business activity of an insured.

   a. The exclusion has several exceptions. For example, it does not apply to occasional or part-time business activities, volunteer activities, and home daycare services not involving compensation or those rendered to a relative.

   b. Although renting property to others qualifies as a business, under the policy definition of business, the exclusion does not apply to occasional rentals of property used as a residence; rental of part of a single-family residence to no more than two roomers or boarders; or rental of property for use only as an office, school, studio, or private garage.

   c. Several endorsements related to home business insurance, business pursuits, and incidental occupancies are available to provide limited liability coverage for certain business activities.

3. Professional Services—Excludes coverage for the insured's rendering or failure to render professional services.

4. Insured's Premises Not an Insured Location—Excludes coverage for bodily injury or property damage arising out of any premises that is owned by or rented to an insured, or that is owned and rented to others by an insured, but is not an insured location.

5. War—Excludes coverage for bodily injury or property damage that results from war.

6. Communicable Disease—Excludes coverage for any claim for any bodily injury or property damage that arises from the transmission of a communicable disease by an insured.

7. Sexual Molestation, Corporal Punishment or Physical or Mental Abuse—Excludes coverage for any loss that arises out of these acts by an insured. Corporal punishment is not defined, but generally refers to spanking, slapping, hitting, and similar disciplinary actions.

8. Controlled Substance—Excludes coverage for any loss that results from the use, sale, manufacture, delivery, transfer, or possession of controlled substances as defined by the Federal Food and Drug Law (such as cocaine, marijuana, and other narcotic drugs, or steroids).

C. Six exclusions apply only to Coverage E—Personal Liability.

1. Loss Assessment and Contractual Liability—Excludes coverage for liability arising from any loss assessment charged against an insured as a member of a homeowners or condominium association or corporation. However, Section II—Additional Coverage provides $1,000 in coverage for this exposure.

2. Damage to the Insured's Property—Excludes coverage for damage to property owned by an insured. The exclusion applies to any costs or expenses an insured incurs to repair, replace, or otherwise modify owned property to prevent injury or damage.

3. Damage to Property in the Insured's Care—Excludes coverage for property rented to, occupied by, or in the care of an insured. An exception to this exclusion applies to property damage caused by fire, smoke, or explosion.

4. Bodily Injury to Persons Eligible for Workers Compensation Benefits—Excludes coverage for bodily injury to any person who is eligible to receive or who is provided benefits by an insured under a state workers compensation law, nonoccupational disability law, or occupational disease law.

5. Nuclear Liability—Excludes bodily injury or property damage liability that would normally be covered under a nuclear energy liability policy.

6. Bodily Injury to an Insured—Excludes coverage of the named insured, resident relatives, and other residents under the age of twenty-one in the insured's care for their own bodily injury, even if the injury is caused by another insured.

D. Four exclusions apply only to Coverage F—Medical Payments to Others.

1. Residence employee off premises—Excludes bodily injury coverage to a residence employee if an injury occurs off the insured's location and the injury does not arise out of the employee's work.

2. Bodily injury eligible for workers compensation benefits—Excludes coverage for any person eligible to receive payment under any workers compensation law, nonoccupational disability law, or occupational disease law.

3. Nuclear reaction—Excludes coverage for bodily injury from any nuclear reaction, nuclear radiation, or radioactive contamination, regardless of the cause.

4. Injury to residents—Excludes bodily injury coverage for any person who regularly resides at the insured location (other than a residence employee).

Educational Objective 3

Summarize each of the HO-3 policy provisions in Section II—Conditions.

Key Points:

Section II—Conditions establishes the insurer's and the insured's duties and responsibilities, including those relating to how claims will be handled. It also describes additional requirements for third parties making claims under Section II. HO-3 Section II—Conditions contains ten conditions:

A. Limit of Liability—This provision stipulates that the limit of Coverage E—Personal Liability on the Declarations page is the total limit of coverage for any one occurrence.

  1. This limit does not increase, regardless of the number of insureds, claims made, or people injured.

  2. The condition also states that all bodily injury and property damage resulting from continuous or repeated exposure to the same harmful conditions are one occurrence, so the Coverage E limit is the maximum paid for any such claim.

  3. The limit of liability applicable to Coverage F—Medical Payments to Others for all medical expenses for bodily injury to one person as the result of an accident cannot exceed the Coverage F limit on the Declarations page.

B. Severability of Insurance—For some occurrences, a claim can involve several insureds. Under this condition, each insured seeking protection is treated as having separate coverage under the policy. The insurer's limit of liability is not increased for any one occurrence if more than one insured is involved.

C. Duties After "Occurrence"—This condition describes several requirements the insured must fulfill if an occurrence occurs under Section II. If the insured does not fully perform these requirements, thus hindering the insurer in performing its duties, the insurer is not obligated to pay the claim. The insured must perform these duties:

  1. Give written notice

  2. Cooperate with the insurer

  3. Forward legal documents

  4. Provide claims assistance

  5. Submit evidence for damage to property of others

  6. Not make voluntary payments

D. Duties of an Insured Person—Coverage F—Medical Payments to Others—This condition stipulates that if an individual (an injured third party) makes a claim for an occurrence under Medical Payments to Others coverage, the injured person (or someone acting on his or her behalf) must fulfill these requirements:

  1. Give the insurer written proof of the claim as soon as possible, under oath if required

  2. Authorize the insurer to obtain copies of medical reports and records

  3. Submit to a physical exam by a doctor chosen by the insurer as often as the insurer requires such examinations

E. Payment of Claim—Coverage F—Medical Payment to Others—This condition stipulates that the insurer's payment of a Medical Payments to Others claim is not an admission of liability by the insured or the insurer. Its purpose is to prevent suits or reduce possible damages resulting from claims by providing prompt payment for injured parties' medical expenses without the need to determine fault.

F. Suit Against Us—This condition states that an insurer cannot be sued under the homeowners policy until certain provisions and terms have been met:

  1. No legal action can be brought against the insurer unless the insured has met all of its Section II obligations.

  2. No one has the right to join the insurer as a party to any action against an insured.

  3. No action with respect to Coverage E can be brought against the insurer until the insured's obligation has been determined by a final judgment or agreement signed by the insurer.

G. Bankruptcy of the Insured—If the insured becomes bankrupt or insolvent, the insurer still must handle the occurrence as it normally would and is not relieved of any policy obligations by the insured's financial status.

H. Other Insurance—Under this condition, limits applicable to any occurrence are excess over any other collectible insurance unless the other insurance specifically provides excess coverage. It differs from the Section I Other Insurance provision, under which any losses are prorated among policies.

I. Policy Period—This condition stipulates that coverage applies only to bodily injury and property damage that occurs during the policy period indicated on the Declarations page.

  1. The claim may be filed at any time, even after policy expiration.

2. The policy does not apply to a claim made during the policy period but involving bodily injury or property damage occurring before the policy's effective date. The policy in effect at the time of the bodily injury or property damage applies.

J. Concealment or Fraud—This provision excludes coverage only for the insured(s) involved in the concealment or fraud, or those making false statements.

1. Other innocent insureds would not be excluded from liability coverage.

2. It differs from the Section I Concealment or Fraud provision, under which concealment or fraud by any insured bars property coverage for all insureds.

Educational Objective 4

Summarize each of the HO-3 policy provisions in Sections I and II—Conditions.

Key Points:

The final section of the Insurance Services Office (ISO) HO-3 homeowners policy includes seven conditions applicable to Sections I and II:

A. The liberalization clause specifies how broadened coverage applies to the policy.
   1. This condition affects only homeowners with the same edition of a policy the insurer subsequently changes.
   2. Any change is effective on the date the insurer makes the coverage change in the state where the insured resides, provided it is made within sixty days before the policy's effective date or within the policy period.
   3. This condition does not apply to changes broadening and restricting coverage in a general homeowners program revision.

B. A waiver or change of provision condition states that only an insurer's written waiver of a right or policy provision change is valid.
   1. The insurer does not waive its rights by asking for an appraisal or an examination.
   2. An insurer can deny coverage after examining all facts associated with a loss or claim.
   3. Courts permit claim representatives' oral waivers during loss adjustment and after a written policy is issued because of their apparent authority.
   4. Insurance agents with binding authority can make policy changes through oral binders, pending a written policy change endorsement.

C. The cancellation condition specifies the requirements for the insured's or the insurer's valid policy termination.
   1. The policyholder may cancel the policy at any time by returning it to the insurer or by writing to the insurer.
   2. Under state regulation, the insurer can cancel the policy only for certain reasons by delivering a written notice to the insured within the stipulated number of days.

3. The premium for the period following the cancellation is calculated on a pro rata basis and refunded to the insured.

4. The insurer may cancel the policy in writing only for these reasons:

   a. For nonpayment of premium if the policyholder has at least ten days' notice before the effective cancellation date

   b. When a new policy has been in effect for fewer than sixty days, for any reason if the policyholder has at least ten days' notice before the cancellation effective date

   c. When the policy has been in effect for more than sixty days (or is a renewal), by giving at least thirty days' notice to the policyholder before the cancellation effective date if a material misrepresentation of fact or substantial risk changed since policy issuance

5. When either party cancels a policy, the insurer sends a refund of the premium to the policyholder with the cancellation notice. Unearned premium is calculated in direct proportion to the portion of the policy term not used.

6. State law often dictates how and when insurers can cancel and nonrenew policies:

   a. When policy language and state laws conflict, state law overrides policy language.

   b. State laws involving cancellation requirements and other matters are often reflected in a state-specific amendatory endorsement to the policy.

D. Under the nonrenewal condition, the insurer can decide not to renew a policy when it expires.

   1. The insurer must provide at least thirty days' written notice of nonrenewal to the insured.

   2. Mailing notice to the address on the declarations is sufficient proof of mailing even if the insured does not receive the notice.

E. The assignment condition states that any assignment of the policy without the insurer's written consent is invalid.

   1. An insurance policy is a personal contract between the insurer and the policyholder, and the insurer must be able to choose whom it will insure.

   2. If an insured property is sold or transferred to another person, the new owner must qualify for a homeowners policy.

F. Subrogation is an insurer's right to recover its claim payment to an insured from the party responsible for the loss.

   1. Subrogation does not apply to the coverages found in Section II—Medical Payments to Others and Damage to Property of Others.

2. If the insured had any rights to collect from another party responsible for the loss, the insurer may require transfer of these rights once it pays a claim to or on behalf of an insured.

3. If another party is ultimately responsible for a loss, the insurer can best pursue any legal remedy required to recover the loss from the responsible party.

4. An insured can, in writing, waive all recovery rights against another person before a loss occurs.

5. The insured does not have the authority after a loss to waive any recovery rights related to that loss.

G. The death condition stipulates that, if the named insured or spouse should die, the insurer agrees to cover the decedent's legal representative (executor or administrator) as an insured only to the extent that the decedent had an interest in the property in the policy.

1. "Insured" includes resident relatives and custodians of the deceased's property as identified in the death condition.

2. The insurer agrees to insure the deceased person's legal representative only with respect to that person's premises and property covered under the homeowners policy at the time of death.

Educational Objective 5

Given a case describing a homeowners liability claim, determine whether the HO-3 policy Section II—Liability Coverages would cover the claim and, if so, the amount the insurer would pay for the claim.

Key Points:

To adequately meet the requirements of this case study's Educational Objective, students should understand the DICE method of policy analysis as well as the specific policy forms and endorsements described in the case to make accurate coverage and loss settlement amount determinations.

To determine whether a policy covers a loss, many insurance professionals apply the DICE method. ("DICE" is an acronym for categories of policy provisions: declarations, insuring agreement, conditions, and exclusions.) The DICE method has four steps:

1. Review of the declarations page to determine whether it covers the person or the property at the time of the loss
2. Review of the insuring agreement to determine whether it covers the loss
3. Review of policy conditions to determine compliance
4. Review of policy exclusions to determine whether they preclude coverage of the loss

Each of these four steps is used in every case. Other categories of policy provisions should be examined. For example, endorsements and terms defined in the policy should be reviewed in relation to the declarations, insuring agreement, exclusions, and conditions.

Key Words and Phrases:

Key Words

Third party
A person or business who is not a party to the insurance contract but who asserts a claim against the insured.

Bodily injury
Physical injury to a person, including sickness, disease, and death.

Property damage
Physical injury to, destruction of, or loss of use of tangible property.

Loss assessment
A charge by the condominium association against the unit owners for the cost of uninsured losses.

Severability of insurance conditions
Policy condition that applies insurance separately to each insured; does not increase the insurer's limit of liability for any one occurrence.

Waiver
The intentional relinquishment of a known right.

Apparent authority
A third party's reasonable belief that an agent has authority to act on the principal's behalf.

Binding authority
An insurance agent's authority to effect coverage on behalf of the insurer.

First-party claim
A demand by an insured person or organization seeking to recover from its insurer for a loss that its insurance policy may cover.

Hold-harmless agreement (or indemnity agreement)
A contractual provision that obligates one of the parties to assume the legal liability of another party.

Homeowners Coverage Forms and Endorsements

7

Key Points:

While the HO-3 policy is the most widely used Insurance Services Office (ISO) homeowners coverage form, numbers HO-2, HO-3, HO-4, HO-5, HO-6, and HO-8 address different situations. The differences among forms are primarily in their Section I—Property Coverages. The remaining sections of the coverage forms are similar, and the Section II—Liability Coverages and Sections I and II—Conditions sections are identical.

Study Tips

Set aside a specific time each day to study.

A. ISO's Homeowners 2—Broad Form (HO 00 02), the HO-2, is designed for the owner-occupant of a house.

   1. An HO-2 has a lower premium than an HO-3 with similar limits because it covers the dwelling and other structures against fewer causes of loss: named perils for personal property, building, and other structures.

   2. Only the HO-2's Section I—Perils Insured Against is different from the HO-3.

      a. The HO-3 provides special form (open perils) coverage for Coverages A and B and named perils coverage for Coverage C.

      b. The HO-2 provides named perils coverage for Coverages A, B, and C.

      c. In both forms, Coverage D is triggered by any loss covered under the other coverages that makes the building unusable.

3. The HO-2's named perils encompass most common insurable perils faced by homeowners; they resemble HO-3 Coverage C named perils.

4. A difference between named perils coverage and special form coverage involves the burden of proof:

    a. With named perils coverage (HO-2), the insured has the burden to prove that the loss was caused by a covered cause of loss for coverage to apply.

    b. With special form coverage (HO-3 Coverages A and B), to deny coverage, the insurer has the burden to prove that the loss was caused by an excluded cause of loss.

B. The Homeowners 5—Comprehensive Form (HO 00 05), the HO-5, provides the broadest property coverage of any of the standard, unendorsed homeowners forms.

    1. The HO-5 is an HO-3 modified to provide special form coverage for the dwelling and other structures and for Coverage C—Personal Property.

    2. The HO-5 covers loss to personal property by any peril.

    3. The HO-5 is subject to the exclusions that apply to Coverages A and B and additional exclusions applicable only to personal property:

        a. Breakage of certain valuable or fragile articles unless caused by a named peril similar to those the HO-3

        b. Damage caused by dampness or temperature extremes unless the direct cause of loss is rain, snow, sleet, or hail

        c. Loss caused by refinishing, renovating, or repairing property other than watches, jewelry, and furs

        d. Loss to personal property caused by collision; other than collision with a land vehicle; or the sinking, swamping, or stranding of watercraft

        e. Government authorities' destruction, confiscation, or seizure of personal property

    4. The HO-5 broadens personal property coverage in some areas simply by not excluding an exposure that has been excluded by the HO-3 policy.

    5. The HO-5 special limits of $1,500 for jewelry and furs, $2,500 for firearms, and $2,500 for silverware apply to items that are stolen and to items that are misplaced or lost. (The HO-3 does not cover misplaced or lost items.)

        a. Lost and misplaced items are subject to a dollar limit, as well as to the policy deductible.

        b. The intentional loss exclusion still applies.

C. ISO's Homeowners 4—Contents Broad Form (HO 00 04), the HO-4, is designed for the needs of persons living in rented houses or apartments.

   1. A homeowner might purchase an HO-4 if the home does not qualify for coverage under another homeowners form.

   2. The HO-4 and the HO-3 provide the same named perils for Coverage C—Personal Property, but the HO-4 differs from the HO-3 in these ways:

      a. Coverages A and B are absent from the HO-4 Section I—Property Coverages; an insured who rents a residence does not typically need coverage on a dwelling or other structure.

      b. HO-4 Coverage C is written at a limit the insured selects as adequate to cover personal property. (In the HO-3, HO-2, and HO-5, the Coverage C limit is typically 50 percent of the Coverage A limit.)

      c. Coverage D in the HO-4 is provided automatically at 30 percent of the Coverage C limit (rather than 30 percent of the Coverage A limit, as in the HO-2 and HO-3).

      d. HO-4 provides an additional coverage for building additions and alterations with a limit up to 10 percent of Coverage C.

      e. HO-4 does not include additional coverage for furnishings provided by a landlord because the occupant-insured of the apartment does not have an insurable interest in such property.

      f. Both the HO-3 and the HO-4 provide additional coverage for "ordinance or law," which would be either a local law (ordinance) or state or federal law imposing new responsibility on a property owner. The HO-3 limit is up to 10 percent of Coverage A. The HO-4 limit is up to 10 percent of the building additions and alterations limit.

D. ISO's Homeowners 6 Unit-Owners Form (HO 00 06), the HO-6, covers the exposures faced by owners of condominium or cooperative units, who jointly own buildings with others and individually own or are responsible for specific units within buildings.

   1. A condominium ownership deed (a condominium declaration, or a master deed) establishes a unit owner's rights.

      a. Such deeds usually contain insurance requirements and describe the insurance provided for the jointly owned property.

b. This insurance might cover a unit owner's entire unit, including the fixtures, plumbing, wiring, or partitions; or it might provide only "bare walls" coverage, applying only to the building structure and walls that support the structure.

2. HO-6 provides coverage for unit owners' property exposures not covered by the condominium insurance. It differs from the HO-3 in these ways:

    a. The HO-6 defines residence premises as the unit where the insured resides. The HO-3 definition includes a one- to four-family dwelling where the insured resides.

    b. The HO-6 description of Coverage A under Section I—Property Coverages includes these items: (1) alterations, appliances, fixtures and improvements that are part of the building contained within the insured unit; (2) items of real property that pertain exclusively to the insured unit; (3) property that is the unit owner's responsibility under a condominium or cooperative association's property owners' agreement; and (4) structures owned solely by the insured at the residence location.

    c. Coverage A—Dwelling in the HO-6 policy provides a basic limit of $5,000. This limit might not be adequate if an insured has extensive property exposures that the condominium association insurance does not cover, and producers often recommend increasing the basic limit.

    d. Coverage B—Other Structures is eliminated from the HO-6 because Coverage A applies to other structures owned solely by the insured.

    e. Coverage C—Personal Property is subject to a limit the insured selects (rather than a percentage of Coverage A).

    f. Coverage D—Loss of Use is provided automatically at a limit that is 50 percent of the Coverage C limit (rather than 30 percent of the Coverage A limit).

    g. Section I—Perils Insured Against in the HO-6 provides named perils coverage for Coverages A and C, similar to the HO-2.

    h. Section I—Conditions in the HO-6 specifies that Coverage A losses are to be settled on a replacement cost basis, as long as the insured makes the repairs "within a reasonable time." HO-6, unlike HO-3, does not require that the Coverage A limit be a percentage of the replacement cost.

3. HO-6 additional coverages also reflect the unique aspects of condominium unit ownership.

    a. Trees, shrubs, and other plants are covered for 10 percent of the Coverage C limit (in contrast to the HO-3 limit of up to 5 percent of the Coverage A) for plants solely owned by the named insured on grounds at the insured unit.

    b. Glass or safety glazing material is covered only if it is part of the insured's unit.

E. ISO's Homeowners 8—Modified Coverage Form (HO 00 08), the HO-8, is for use where the replacement cost of an owner-occupied dwelling significantly exceeds its market value, such as a large, older house with obsolete construction or features that would be expensive to replace.

1. Many insurers are unwilling to write an HO-3 in this situation because it creates a moral hazard.

2. The HO-8 Section I—Conditions specifies that if the insured makes repairs after a loss, the insurer will not pay more than the cost of "common construction materials and methods" that are "functionally equivalent to and less costly than obsolete, antique, or custom construction."

Educational Objective 2

Summarize the coverages provided by various ISO homeowners policy endorsements.

Key Points:

A homeowners policy coverage may be modified through these common Insurance Services Office (ISO) endorsements to fit the insured's needs:

A. The Inflation Guard endorsement (HO 04 46) helps prevent underinsurance caused by economic inflation and rising replacement costs.

    1. The endorsement gradually and automatically increases limits throughout the policy period for Section I Property Coverages A, B, C, and D.

    2. The insured and the insurer agree annually on a percentage of increase, such as 4, 6, or 8 percent, that is applied to the original amount of insurance. Additional 4 percent increments are available.

B. The Scheduled Personal Property Endorsement (HO 04 61) covers personal property for which an unendorsed homeowners policy does not provide adequate protection.

    1. This endorsement provides scheduled coverage for specific items, including jewelry, furs, cameras, musical instruments, silverware, golfer's equipment, fine arts, postage stamps, and rare and current coins.

    2. Neither the Coverage C special limits nor the Section I deductible apply to scheduled items.

C. The Personal Property Replacement Cost Loss Settlement endorsement (HO 04 90) provides replacement cost coverage on personal property, awnings, carpeting, household appliances, and outdoor equipment. Without this endorsement, losses to personal property are settled on an actual cash value basis.

    1. This endorsement lists types of property ineligible for replacement cost coverage, including rare articles that cannot be replaced, articles whose age or history contribute to their value, articles not maintained, and outdated and obsolete articles.

    2. For items covered under the endorsement, the insurer will pay no more than the least of these values:

        a. Replacement cost at the time of loss, without deduction for depreciation

       b. Full cost of repair at the time of loss

       c. Limit of liability applicable to Coverage C—Personal Property

       d. Any applicable special limits of liability in the policy

       e. Limit of liability for loss that applies to any item separately described and specifically insured under the policy

    3. For losses with a replacement value of more than $500, the insured must repair or replace the lost or damaged items before the insurer will pay the replacement cost.

D. The Personal Injury endorsement (HO 24 82) expands homeowners liability coverage by adding the definition of personal injury and adding personal injury coverage.

    1. Personal injuries are injuries arising out of one or more of these offenses:

       a. False arrest, detention, or imprisonment

       b. Malicious prosecution

       c. Invasion of privacy, wrongful eviction, or wrongful entry

       d. Libel or slander against a person or organization or disparaging acts against a person's or organization's goods, products, or services

       e. Libel or slander that violates a person's right of privacy

    2. Exclusions relate to intentional acts, criminal acts, contractual liability, employment, business activities, bodily injury to an insured, civic or public activities performed for pay, and pollutants.

E. The Home Business Insurance Coverage, or HOMEBIZ, endorsement (HO 07 01) provides a comprehensive business package policy, when attached to a homeowners form, for insureds who operate an office or a service, sales, or crafts business from their homes.

    1. This endorsement provides a wider range of coverages normally found only in a commercial insurance policy.

    2. The endorsement excludes professional liability coverage and lists many excluded professional activities.

    3. Insurers determine final underwriting eligibility, but the policy lists the minimum requirements for coverage of a home business:

       a. The business must be owned by an insured or a business entity comprising only the insured and resident relatives.

       b. It must be operated from the residence premises identified on the homeowners Declarations page, and the residence premises must be used primarily for residential purposes.

       c. It can have up to three employees.

      d. It cannot involve the manufacture, sale, or distribution of food products.

      e. It cannot involve the manufacture of personal care products such as shampoo, soap, perfume, hair color, or similar items.

      f. It cannot involve the sale or distribution of personal care products manufactured by the insured.

      g. It cannot have gross annual receipts exceeding $250,000.

  4. This home business endorsement provides these coverages:

      a. Section I—Property Coverage provides full Coverage C—Personal Property limits for business property, accounts receivable ($5,000 limit), loss of business income and extra expense (actual cost for a maximum of twelve months), and valuable papers ($2,500 limit) and increases the Coverage C—Personal Property special limits on money ($1,000), credit cards ($1,000), and business property away from the premises ($5,000).

      b. Section II—Liability Coverages provides products-completed operations coverage up to an annual aggregate limit equal to the Coverage E—Personal Liability limit; provides all other business liability coverage (including personal and advertising injury but not professional liability) up to an annual aggregate of twice the combined Coverage E—Personal Liability and Coverage F—Medical Payments to Others limits; provides medical payments coverage equal to the Coverage F—limit; and increases the Damage to Property of Others limit to $2,500.

F. The Earthquake endorsement (HO 04 54) provides coverage for damage caused by earthquake and land shock waves caused by volcanic eruption.

G. The Ordinance or Law—Increased Amount of Coverage endorsement (HO 04 77) covers the costs of a homeowner's repairs made after a loss to comply with current ordinances or laws. It increases the HO-3 limit for such costs (10 percent of the Coverage A—Dwelling limit) in increments of 25 percent, up to an unlimited percentage of the Coverage A limit.

H. The Water Back Up and Sump Discharge or Overflow endorsement (HO 04 95) adds $5,000 of property coverage for water or waterborne materials backed up through sewers or drains or overflowing from a sump pump, pump, or related equipment. A deductible of $250 applies to this endorsement.

I. The Loss Assessment Coverage endorsement (HO 04 35) adds coverage to the Additional Coverages of Section I—Property Coverages and Section II—Liability Coverages for insureds living in communities with neighborhood associations who are charged monthly fees to cover the costs of the maintenance and upkeep of the common areas of the neighborhoods.

   1. The endorsement sets a limit of $1,000 on an assessment that is applied to the association's insurance deductible.

   2. The endorsement applies to loss resulting from a single event, whether it involves property, liability, or both.

J. The Additional Residence Rented to Others—1, 2, 3, or 4 Families endorsement (HO 24 70) covers insureds who own rental property not at the insured location. It extends Coverage E—Personal Liability and Coverage F—Medical Payments to Others to these insureds.

K. The Credit Card, Electronic Fund Transfer Card or Access Device, Forgery, and Counterfeit Money—Increased Limit endorsement (HO 04 53) increases the limit in homeowners policies' Section I for losses resulting from the unauthorized use of an insured's credit card, bank transfer card, check forgery, or acceptance of counterfeit money. It adds coverage to as much as a $10,000 limit.

L. The Limited Fungi, Wet or Dry Rot, or Bacteria Coverage endorsement (HO 04 26 04 02) provides coverage for losses caused by mold.

   1. It includes mold in the definition of fungi, covers mold losses unless the mold results from fighting a fire, and restricts coverage for repeated seepage.

   2. It also limits coverage to $10,000 for loss from mold arising from a covered water loss. The insured can elect to increase this limit or to increase the annual aggregate limit of $50,000 on mold liability claims.

Educational Objective 3

Given a case describing a homeowners claim, determine whether an HO-3 Policy (endorsed or unendorsed) would cover the claim, and if so, the amount the insurer would pay for the claim.

Key Points:

To adequately meet the requirements of this case study's Educational Objective, students should understand the DICE method of policy analysis as well as the specific policy forms and endorsements described in the case to make accurate coverage and loss settlement amount determinations.

Apply the steps in the DICE method to the specific issues of the coverage claim.

To determine whether a policy covers a loss, many insurance professionals apply the DICE method. ("DICE" is an acronym for categories of policy provisions: declarations, insuring agreement, conditions, and exclusions.) The DICE method has four steps:

1. Review of the declarations page to determine whether it covers the person or the property at the time of the loss

2. Review of the insuring agreement to determine whether it covers the loss

3. Review of policy conditions to determine compliance

4. Review of policy exclusions to determine whether they preclude coverage of the loss

Each of these four steps is used in every case. Other categories of policy provisions should be examined. For example, endorsements and terms defined in the policy should be reviewed in relation to the declarations, insuring agreement, exclusions, and conditions.

Key Words and Phrases:

Burden of proof
In a trial, the duty of a party to prove that the facts it claims are true.

Condominium or cooperative units
Housing unit in a complex owned by a corporation, the stockholders of which are the building's residents; the corporation owns the real estate title; each unit owner owns corporation stock and has the right to occupy a specific unit.

Moral hazard
A condition that increases the likelihood that a person will intentionally cause or exaggerate a loss.

Scheduled coverage
Insurance for property specifically listed (scheduled) on a policy, with a limit of liability for each item.

Other Residential Insurance

8

Educational Objective 1

Contrast the DP-3 policy with the HO-3 policy in regard to each of the following:

- **Types of property covered**

- **Other coverages**

- **Perils insured against**

- **Exclusions and conditions**

- **Coverage for liability and theft losses**

Key Points:

An insured who might not want, need, or wish to pay for full homeowners policy coverages can choose to buy a dwelling policy.

A. A dwelling policy can cover owner- and nonowner-occupied dwellings.

    1. The HO-3 policy covers owner-occupied one- to four-family dwellings, while dwelling policies insure owner-occupied or tenant-occupied one- to four-family dwellings.

    2. Dwelling policies can cover four other kinds of property and activities:

        a. A dwelling in the course of construction

        b. Mobile homes at a permanent location

        c. Houseboats in some states

        d. Certain incidental business occupancies if operated by the owner-insured or a tenant of the insured location

    3. Unlike the HO-3 policy, the dwelling policy does not automatically include all the property coverages. A limit for each desired coverage (dwelling, other structures, and personal property) must appear on the Declarations page.

Study Tips

Remember to register for your exam by calling The Institutes at (800) 644-2101.

B. The DP-3 offers coverage for a dwelling and its contents that is similar to coverages under homeowners forms Section I (property). It includes five coverages:

1. Coverage A—Dwelling covers the dwelling on the described location shown in the declarations and specifies that it must be used principally for dwelling purposes.

   a. The HO-3 form refers to the dwelling on the residence premises, including attached structures.

   b. The dwelling form states that, if not covered elsewhere in the policy, building equipment and outdoor equipment used for the service of the premises and located on the described location are covered.

2. Coverage B—Other Structures in the DP-3 form is essentially the same as that in the HO-3 form.

   a. As in the HO-3 policy, Coverage B includes detached structures, such as garages and storage sheds, on the insured premises.

   b. Gravemarkers and mausoleums are specifically excluded under Other Structures in the DP-3 form, whereas the HO-3 policy provides up to $5,000 for gravemarkers as an additional coverage.

3. Coverage C—Personal Property, if selected, applies to personal property usual to the occupancy of a dwelling that the insured or resident family members own or use, while the property is on the described location.

4. Coverage D—Fair rental value covers the fair rental value of a property rented to others when it becomes unfit for its normal use because of a loss by a covered peril.

5. Coverage E—Increased Living Expenses covers the insured's increased living expenses if the described property becomes unfit for its normal use because of loss by a covered peril.

C. Other Coverages—Many dwelling policy coverages correspond to the additional coverages in the homeowners policy, but with some differences.

1. Loss assessment coverage, included automatically (up to $1,000) in the homeowners policy, can be added to the dwelling policy by endorsement for an additional premium.

2. The additional coverages in the homeowners policy for landlord's furnishings and credit cards, transfer cards, forgery, and counterfeit money are not available in the dwelling policy.

3. The DP-3 form provides up to 10 percent of the Coverage A limit for Coverage B—Other Structures as additional insurance.

4. The DP-3 debris removal coverage is included in the limit applicable to damaged property. Unlike the HO-3, the DP-3 form does not cover debris removal for trees, shrubs, and plants.

5. The DP-3 form provides 10 percent of the Coverage C limit as additional insurance to cover a tenant's improvements, alterations, and additions for loss by a covered peril. The HO-3 form has no comparable coverage.

6. The DP-3 form provides up to 10 percent of the Coverage C limit for loss to the property covered under Coverage C, except rowboats and canoes, anywhere in the world. The HO-3 form has no such limitation, except for property usually located at an insured's secondary residence.

7. The DP-3 form provides up to 20 percent of the Coverage A limit for losses under both Coverage D—Fair Rental Value and Coverage E—Additional Living Expense. Under the HO-3 form, the corresponding additional limit for loss of use is 30 percent of the Coverage A limit.

8. The DP-3 form, like the HO-3 form, provides coverage for the cost of reasonable repairs made after the occurrence of a covered loss solely to protect covered property from further damage. This coverage does not increase the limit of liability applicable to the covered property.

9. Under both the DP-3 and HO-3, covered property is protected if it is removed from the premises because it is endangered by an insured peril.

10. In both the HO-3 and the DP-3 forms, the maximum limit that can be applied (as additional insurance) to trees, shrubs, other plants, or lawns is 5 percent of the Coverage A limit.

11. The DP-3 form, like the HO-3 form, will pay up to $500 for fire department service charges if fire protection is not otherwise provided. This coverage is additional insurance, and no deductible applies.

12. The DP-3 form offers coverage for building collapse resulting from specified perils. Collapse coverage does not increase the limit of liability that applies to the damaged covered property.

13. The DP-3 form provides coverage for breakage of glass or safety glazing material that is part of a building, storm door, or storm window, and for damage to covered property caused by the breakage. Similar coverage is included in the HO-3 form.

14. The DP-3 form provides coverage for increased costs the insured incurs because of the enforcement of any ordinance or law. Coverage is provided up to 10 percent of the Coverage A limit, or, if there is no Coverage A limit, up to 10 percent of the Coverage B limit. This coverage is additional insurance. If the insured is a tenant at the described location, the limit is up to 10 percent of the limit that applies to improvements, alterations, and additions.

D. Perils Insured Against—The DP-3, like the HO-3, uses the special form approach and insures against "risk of direct loss to property" (as opposed to named perils coverage) under Coverage A—Dwelling and Coverage B—Other Structures. Although the Coverage C named perils under the DP-3 form are similar to the named perils coverage in the HO-3 form, there are some differences.

1. The DP-3 does not cover theft of personal property, but it covers damage to covered property caused by burglars unless the dwelling has been vacant for more than thirty days.

2. The DP-3 specifically excludes pilferage, theft, burglary, and larceny under the peril of vandalism or malicious mischief.

3. The DP-3 specifically excludes wind or hail damage to canoes and rowboats; the HO-3 covers such damage to watercraft and their trailers, furnishings, equipment, and outboard motors, but only while the items are inside a fully enclosed building.

E. Exclusions and Conditions

1. The general exclusions in the DP-3 track closely with the Section I exclusions in the HO-3 and include loss caused directly or indirectly by several perils or events:

   a. Ordinance or law, except as provided in the Other Coverages section

   b. Earth movement, such as an earthquake

   c. Water damage, such as flood and backup of sewers and drains

   d. Power failure that occurs off the described location

   e. Neglect on the part of the insured

   f. War

   g. Nuclear hazard

   h. Intentional loss

   i. Weather conditions that contribute to any of the preceding excluded causes of loss

   j. Acts or decisions of other persons, groups, organizations, or governmental bodies

   k. Faulty construction, planning, materials, or maintenance

    2. The DP-3 form contains a single section of conditions. These conditions include the insured's duties after a loss, loss to a pair or set, other insurance, mortgage clause, and other similar conditions regarding the coverage.

F. Although the ISO dwelling forms do not provide coverage for liability or theft losses, such coverages are available by adding a personal liability supplement and a theft endorsement.

    1. Liability coverage may be written as an addendum to the dwelling policy or as a separate policy using the personal liability supplement (DL 24 01).

        a. An insured who has both a homeowners policy on his or her residence and a dwelling policy on a rental dwelling can obtain liability coverage for the rental dwelling by purchasing the homeowners additional residence rented to others endorsement (HO 24 70) for an additional premium.

        b. The personal liability supplement provides Coverage L—Personal Liability and Coverage M—Medical Payments to Others.

        c. The exclusions and additional coverages in the personal liability supplement are virtually the same as those applicable to Section II of the homeowners policy. However, the HO-3 additional liability coverage for loss assessment provided (up to a limit of $1,000) is not provided in the personal liability supplement.

    2. An insured may choose between two endorsements to the dwelling form to provide theft coverage similar to that provided in the homeowners policy.

        a. The Broad Theft Coverage (DP 04 72) endorsement covers theft, including attempted theft, and vandalism or malicious mischief as a result of theft or attempted theft on-premises and off-premises. Off-premises coverage is available only if the insured purchases on-premises coverage. The endorsement includes special limits similar to the sublimits included in the HO-3 form, such as those for money, jewelry, and firearms.

        b. The Limited Theft Coverage (DP 04 73) endorsement covers only on-premises theft, attempted theft, and vandalism or malicious mischief as a result of theft or attempted theft. The endorsement includes special limits only for watercraft and their trailers, trailers not used for watercraft, and firearms and related equipment. It does not cover off-premises theft.

Educational Objective 2

Given a case describing a dwelling claim, determine whether the DP-3 policy would cover the claim and, if so, the amount the insurer would pay for the claim.

Key Points:

To adequately meet the requirements of this case study's Educational Objective, students should understand the DICE method of policy analysis as well as the specific policy forms and endorsements described in the case to make accurate coverage and loss settlement amount determinations.

To determine whether a policy covers a loss, many insurance professionals apply the DICE method. ("DICE" is an acronym for categories of policy provisions: declarations, insuring agreement, conditions, and exclusions.) The DICE method has four steps:

1. Review of the declarations page to determine whether it covers the person or the property at the time of the loss
2. Review of the insuring agreement to determine whether it covers the loss
3. Review of policy conditions to determine compliance
4. Review of policy exclusions to determine whether they preclude coverage of the loss

Each of these four steps is used in every case. Other categories of policy provisions should be examined. For example, endorsements and terms defined in the policy should be reviewed in relation to the declarations, insuring agreement, exclusions, and conditions.

Educational Objective 3

Explain how the coverages under the HO-3 policy are modified by the Mobilehome Endorsement (MH 04 01) and other ISO endorsements unique to mobilehome coverage.

Key Points:

Mobilehomes are less expensive than homes on permanent foundations, are often on leased land, and create special needs for coverage. The ISO Mobilehome Endorsement modifies homeowners policies to provide such coverage, and additional endorsements can further customize coverage.

A. A mobilehome owner might experience loss from typical exposures also faced by conventional homeowners (such as damage to or destruction of the mobilehome and to personal property, loss of use of the mobilehome, and liability losses), as well as additional exposures.

   1. Because of construction materials and loose foundations, mobilehomes are vulnerable to damage from windstorms, tornadoes, and earthquakes.

      a. Mobilehomes' wheels are removed when the structure is set on blocks, piers, or masonry footings.

      b. Some state codes require that mobilehomes be tied down, and many insurers provide mobilehome coverage only if the structure is properly tied down.

      c. Skirting material attached to the bottom of a mobilehome to give the appearance of a permanent structure also reduces the buildup of debris and helps prevent damage.

   2. Because of their use as vacation homes, mobilehomes may be located in recreational areas subject to greater loss exposure and the absence of services.

   3. The contents of mobilehomes and other structures are usually similar to those in conventional dwellings and are subject to the same exposures. Mobilehomes often have built-in cabinets, appliances, and furniture that are considered part of the mobilehome rather than personal property.

B. The ISO Mobilehome Endorsement (MH 04 01) can be added to an HO-3 or HO-2 policy.

   1. A mobilehome is eligible for coverage if it is designed for portability and year-round living, is at least ten feet wide, and has an area of at least four hundred square feet.

2. A mobilehome policy is created by attaching the Mobilehome Endorsement to a homeowners form and a Declarations page. Other endorsements may be attached to modify the coverage.

3. The mobilehome policy modifies the HO-3 policy in several ways:

   a. Definitions—"Residence premises" means the mobilehome and other structures located on land owned or leased by the insured where the insured resides.

   b. Section I—Property Coverages, Coverage A—Dwelling—This coverage applies to a mobilehome used primarily as a private residence and to attached structures and utility tanks. It also applies to floor coverings, appliances, and similar items that are permanently installed and to materials and supplies (located on or next to the residence premises) for construction, alteration, or repair of the mobilehome or other structures on that premises.

   c. Section I—Property Coverages, Coverage B—Other Structures—The liability coverage limit for other structures on the premises is a maximum of 10 percent of the limit that applies to Coverage A, with a minimum limit of $2,000.

   d. Section I—Property Coverages, Additional Coverages—"Property removed" coverage provides up to $500 (with no deductible) for removal and return of a mobilehome to avoid damage by an insured peril. The Mobilehome Endorsement removes the "ordinance or law" additional coverage in the HO-3; however, it may be restored by another endorsement.

   e. Section I—Conditions, Loss Settlement—Carpeting and appliances are not included as property to be valued on the basis of actual cash value. Such property is included in Coverage A, and replacement cost coverage applies.

   f. Section I—Conditions, Loss to a Pair or Set—Additional coverage is available to repair or replace damaged parts of a series of panels to match the remainder of the panels.

   g. Section I—Conditions, Mortgage Clause—This provision modifies the word "mortgagee" in the policy to include a lienholder.

4. The Mobilehome Endorsement amends the homeowners policy's Section I—Property Coverages. It does not amend Section II—Liability Coverages.

C. A mobilehome policy can be endorsed with many typical homeowners endorsements. Five such endorsements are available only for the mobilehome policy.

1. The Actual Cash Value Mobilehome endorsement (MH 04 02) changes the loss settlement terms on the mobilehome and other structures to apply an actual cash value (ACV) basis rather than a replacement cost basis.

2. The Transportation/Permission to Move endorsement (MH 04 03) provides coverage for perils of transportation (collision, upset, stranding, or sinking) and for the mobilehome and other structures at the new location anywhere in the United States or Canada for thirty days from the effective date of the endorsement.

3. The Mobilehome Lienholder's Single Interest endorsement (MH 04 04) provides coverage only to the lienholder for collision and upset transportation exposures, subject to numerous recovery conditions, and for any loss resulting from the owner's conversion, embezzlement, or secretion (concealment) of the mobilehome. Some lienholders require this endorsement.

4. The Property Removed Increased Limit endorsement (MH 04 06) allows the policyholder to increase the Mobilehome Endorsement's $500 limit for removing a mobilehome endangered by an insured peril.

5. The Ordinance or Law Coverage endorsement (MH 04 08), identical to the Ordinance or Law additional coverage provision in the homeowners policy, enables the mobilehome policyholder to add this coverage for an amount equal to a specified percentage of the Coverage A limit.

Educational Objective 4

Describe the operation of the National Flood Insurance Program and the coverage it provides.

Key Points:

Both homeowners and dwelling policies exclude flood losses. To make flood insurance available to property owners, the federal government provides it through the National Flood Insurance Program (NFIP) at subsidized rates for both dwellings and commercial buildings, as well as for the contents of both.

A. Community Eligibility

1. Flood insurance may be written only in communities that the Federal Emergency Management Agency (FEMA) has designated as participating communities in the NFIP.

2. A community's residents become eligible for flood insurance in one of two ways:

    a. The community applies to the Federal Insurance Administration (FIA) to be included in the NFIP.

    b. FEMA determines that an area is flood-prone and notifies the community that it has one year to decide whether to join the NFIP.

    - The FIA notifies those communities and offers to help deal with their flood problems should they elect to join the NFIP.

    - A community that chooses not to join the NFIP is not eligible for federal flood assistance.

3. If a community identified as flood-prone does not wish to participate in the NFIP, it has two options:

    a. Contest the designation

    A community that successfully contests the flood-prone designation is still eligible for federal aid if a flood occurs.

    b. Choose not to participate

    If a community chooses not to participate in the NFIP, its access to federal funds is limited.

4. Some states require NFIP participation as part of their flood-plain management program.

B. Incentives and Programs

1. A community that includes a special flood hazard area (SFHA) must participate in the NFIP program for NFIP flood insurance to be available within that community.

2. The law restricts development by prohibiting any form of federal financial assistance for acquisition or construction purposes in an SFHA unless the community participates in NFIP.

3. If a disaster occurs as a result of flooding in a nonparticipating community, no federal financial assistance can be provided for the permanent repair or reconstruction of insurable buildings in SFHAs.

4. Emergency program

   a. Once a community has submitted an application for flood insurance and all other necessary information to the FIA, the FIA prepares a flood hazard boundary map if one does not exist.

   - It identifies the SFHAs within a community.
   - The map defines areas where people in SFHAs can buy coverages.
   - The map is used in the NFIP's emergency program for floodplain management and insurance purposes.

   b. When a community first joins the NFIP, property owners in special flood hazard areas can purchase limited amounts of insurance at subsidized rates under the emergency program.

   c. The FIA arranges for a detailed study of the community and its susceptibility to flood, which results in a Flood Insurance Rate Map (FIRM) that divides the community into specific zones to identify the probability of flooding in each zone.

   - The amount of coverage is based on the type of building or contents, and emergency premium rates only apply for residential buildings, for residential contents, for nonresidential buildings, and for nonresidential contents.
   - These rates, which apply per $100 of insurance, are uniform in all eligible communities. The maximum limits are $35,000 for a single- or two- to four-family dwelling and $10,000 for its contents.

   d. Once the first layer of insurance coverage has been made available to individuals in a flood-prone area through the emergency program, they cannot obtain federal or federally insured loans for new construction unless they purchase flood insurance.

5. Regular program

   a. After FEMA completes its assessment of a community's flood-prone area, establishes an accurate FIRM, and calculates actuarial rates, the community is promoted from the emergency program to the second and final NFIP phase, the regular program.

   b. The maximum limits of coverage are $250,000 for a single- or two- to four-family dwelling and $100,000 for its contents, with variations for nonresidential buildings.

   c. The conversion from the emergency program to the regular program depends on the community's enacting and enforcing floodplain management regulations. A community that fails to convert is suspended from the program.

C. Flood Insurance Coverage

 1. Three flood insurance policies

   All three available policies protect insureds against direct losses to real and personal property from the flood peril. These policies do not cover indirect losses.

   a. The dwelling form is used for any dwelling having an occupancy of no more than four families.

   b. The general property form is used for all other occupancies—that is, multi-residential and nonresidential, except for residential condominium building associations.

   c. Residential condominium building associations are eligible for coverage under the residential condominium building association form.

 2. Waiting period

   a. To avoid adverse selection, the NFIP generally requires a thirty-day waiting period for new flood insurance policies and for endorsements that increase coverage on existing policies.

   b. An exception to the waiting period is made for flood insurance that is purchased initially in connection with a property purchase or a new or an increased mortgage on a property.

 3. Write-your-own (WYO) program

   a. The NFIP provides government-underwritten flood insurance through two mechanisms:

   - A producer may write the business directly through the servicing representative designated by the FIA.
   - A producer may place the business with an insurer participating in FIA's Write-Your-Own (WYO) program.

   b. Insurers participating in the WYO program issue the majority (more than 90 percent) of NFIP policies in force.

   c. WYO allows private insurers participating in the program to sell and service flood insurance under their own names.

    d. Regardless of whether the NFIP or a WYO insurer issues a policy, the coverage provided is identical, and WYO insurers use exactly the same language used in policies that the NFIP issues directly.

    e. In the WYO program, the FIA determines rates, coverage limitations, and eligibility. The NFIP totally reinsures the coverage.

- Insurers receive an expense allowance for policies written and claims processed, while the federal government retains responsibility for losses.

- Insurers collect premiums, retain commissions, and use the remainder of the premiums to pay claims.

    f. If flood losses exceed the amounts an insurer holds to pay flood claims, the federal government makes up the difference. However, if flood insurance premiums exceed losses, the insurer pays the excess to the federal government.

D. Flood Insurance Reform

    1. The Flood Insurance Reform Act of 2004 reformed the NFIP and the terms of the National Flood Insurance Act.

    2. It created a five-year pilot program to reduce losses to properties experiencing repetitive flood insurance claims (four or more flood insurance claim payments of more than $5,000 each, with the cumulative amount exceeding $20,000, or two or more claim payments that cumulatively exceed the value of the property).

    3. The reform act's preamble included Congressional findings that quantify the motivation behind the act, such as the cost to taxpayers (about $200 million annually).

    4. This act provided a disincentive to property owners to live in repetitively flooded areas.

        a. Rather than encouraging rebuilding, the program provides repeatedly flooded homeowners with assistance in either elevating or moving their homes away from flood waters.

        b. Most mitigation offers involve elevation assistance.

        c. Refusal of a mitigation offer triggers rate increases.

    5. The act reduces intensive development in repeatedly flooded areas to help restore the natural functions of floodplains, such as wildlife biodiversity and wetlands that absorb flood waters.

Educational Objective 5

Describe the operation of FAIR plans and beachfront and windstorm plans and the coverage they provide.

Key Points:

State governments have developed Fair Access to Insurance Requirements (FAIR) plans and beachfront and windstorm plans, enabling homeowners to purchase insurance for urban and coastal properties that are not insurable in the voluntary insurance market.

A. FAIR plans make standard lines of property insurance available for exposures in areas underserved by the voluntary market.

    1. Participating private insurers and state insurance authorities coordinate efforts to provide such coverage.

    2. Each state with a FAIR plan has enacted its own legislation in response to local market needs, so the coverage provided and the methods of operation vary considerably.

    3. FAIR plans make insurance coverage available when insurers in the voluntary market cannot profitably provide coverage at a reasonable rate for policyholders and provide the needed support for credit, as in these examples:

        a. Property in urban areas susceptible to damage caused by riots and civil commotion

        b. Coastal properties that pose greater-than-average exposure to windstorm damage

        c. Homes in wooded, suburban areas with the potential hazard of brush fires

    4. A property owner can apply for insurance to the state's FAIR plan through an authorized insurance agent or broker.

        a. The FAIR plan might operate as a policy-issuing syndicate, in which the plan issues the policies and the plan's staff handles underwriting, processing, and possibly claim handling.

        b. In several states, the FAIR plan contracts with one or more voluntary insurers to act as servicing organizations. For a percentage of premium, these insurers perform underwriting, policyholder service, and claim handling functions.

        c. In the majority of plans, all licensed property insurers must share payment for plan losses in proportion to their share of property insurance premiums collected within the state.

5. To be eligible for FAIR plan coverage, a property must be ineligible for coverage in the voluntary market, and the policyholder must have the property inspected by the FAIR plan administrator. Only property that meets the FAIR plan inspection criteria can be insured through the program.

   a. If the property fails to meet the basic safety levels, owners can be required to make improvements as a condition for obtaining insurance.

   b. If the problems are not corrected, the state can deny insurance, provided the exposures are not related to the neighborhood location or to hazardous environmental conditions that are beyond the owner's control.

6. Under most FAIR plans, five types of exposures are considered uninsurable:

   a. Property that is vacant or open to trespass

   b. Property that is poorly maintained or that has unrepaired fire damage

   c. Property that is subject to unacceptable physical hazards

   d. Property that violates a law or public policy

   e. In some states, property that was not built in accordance with building and safety codes

7. Some state FAIR plans provide limited homeowners coverage; however, most plans provide coverage only for fire and a limited number of perils, which often include vandalism, riot, and windstorm.

   a. Available insurance limits and mandatory deductibles vary widely among plans.

   b. When a policyholder wants greater coverage than that offered by the FAIR plan, a specialty insurer can write a difference in conditions policy (DIC).

B. Beachfront and windstorm plans are similar to FAIR plans in that they make insurance coverage available for properties with greater-than-average exposure to loss and provide the needed support for credit.

   1. Most beachfront and windstorm plans provide insurance coverage for windstorm and hail losses that cannot be obtained in the voluntary market.

   2. Under these plans, losses from tidal water are generally excluded and should be covered under a flood insurance policy.

   3. The operation of beachfront and windstorm plans is similar to that of FAIR plans.

      a. Some states use a single servicing organization that provides the underwriting, policyholder services, and claim handling services.

    b. Others operate as policy-issuing syndicates in which the plan issues the policies and the plan's staff provides services.

    c. In all plans, insurers that write property coverages in that state must share in plan losses in proportion to their share of state property insurance premiums.

4. Properties eligible for coverage under beachfront and windstorm plans must be ineligible for coverage in the voluntary market and must be located in designated coastal areas.

    a. In some states, the property must be located within a certain distance of the shoreline.

    b. Owners of property in coastal areas can obtain coverage for most real and personal property through these plans.

    c. Eligibility for coverage under each plan requires that buildings constructed or rebuilt after a specified date conform to an applicable building code.

    d. In addition to dwellings and other residential buildings, mobile homes may be eligible if they meet certain construction and tie-down requirements.

5. As with FAIR plans, beachfront and windstorm plans will not insure certain types of property:

    a. Property that is poorly maintained or that has unrepaired damage

    b. Property that is subject to poor housekeeping

    c. Property that violates a law or public policy

6. The perils insured against in beachfront and windstorm plans vary by state, but many such plans provide only windstorm and hail coverage.

    a. In those states, policyholders must obtain other property coverages through the voluntary insurance market or other nonstandard markets.

    b. The maximum limits of insurance available, as well as deductibles, vary among states.

    c. State plans generally contain a provision that no application for new coverage or increase in limits will be accepted when a hurricane has formed within a certain distance of the beach area where the property is located.

7. In recent years, some states have merged their FAIR and beachfront and windstorm plans.

    a. Florida and Louisiana have merged their FAIR and windstorm plans to create state-run property insurance companies.

    b. These state plans provide coverage for a range of exposures throughout the state; however, the primary loss exposure is beachfront windstorms.

Key Words and Phrases:

Key Words

Special flood hazard area (SFHA)
Area that the NFIP has classified as being expected to experience flooding at least once in 100 years.

Flood hazard boundary map
A temporary map designed to identify flood-prone areas in the community.

Emergency program
Initial phase of a community's participation in the National Flood Insurance Program in which property owners in flood areas can purchase limited amounts of insurance at subsidized rates.

Flood Insurance Rate Map (FIRM)
A map that shows exact boundaries for special flood hazard areas, the various flood zones, and base flood elevations.

Regular program
Second phase of the National Flood Insurance Program in which the community agrees to adopt flood-control and land-use restrictions and in which property owners purchase higher amounts of flood insurance than under the emergency program.

Write-Your-Own (WYO) program
A program allowing private insurers to write flood insurance under the National Flood Insurance Program (NFIP).

Syndicate
A group of insurers or reinsurers involved in joint underwriting to insure major risks that are beyond the capacity of a single insurer or reinsurer; each syndicate member accepts predetermined shares of premiums, losses, expenses, and profits.

Difference in conditions (DIC) policy, or DIC insurance
Policy that covers on an "all-risks" basis to fill gaps in the insured's commercial property coverage, especially gaps in flood and earthquake coverage.

Other Personal Property and Liability Insurance

Educational Objective 1

Summarize the coverages provided by personal inland marine policies.

Key Points:

A homeowners policy may not provide adequate insurance for some types of personal property. Often, such coverage needs can be met with a personal inland marine policy. Inland marine insurance is designed to cover property that has special value or that frequently moves ("floats") from one location to another.

Study Tips

Have you reviewed the answers to the review questions?

A. Personal inland marine policies can provide higher limits of insurance than those of homeowners personal property coverages for losses of a particular type or that occur at a particular location.

   1. Although they can be customized to meet a variety of coverage needs, personal inland marine policies share these characteristics:

   a. The coverage is tailored to the specific type of property to be insured, such as a musical instrument.

   b. The insured may select the appropriate policy limits.

   c. Policies are often written without a deductible.

   d. Most policies insure property worldwide with special form coverage (open perils), subject to exclusions.

   2. Personal inland marine policies have a shared structure consisting of three components:

   a. Declarations page

   b. Common policy provisions

   c. Coverage form

B. The Common Policy Provisions of the ISO personal inland marine policy include an insuring agreement, definitions, exclusions, and conditions.

   1. The insuring agreement states that the insurer provides the insurance in return for the premium paid by the insured and the insured's compliance with policy provisions.

   2. Exclusions apply to losses caused by these perils:

   a. War

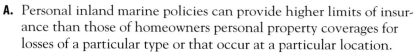

     b. Nuclear hazard

     c. Governmental action

     d. Intentional loss

     e. Neglect

3. The Conditions section specifies that insured property may have scheduled coverage by which items are specifically listed. Generally, the amount paid for a covered loss is the least of four amounts:

     a. The actual cash value of the insured property at the time of loss

     b. The amount for which the insured property could be repaired

     c. The amount for which the insured property could be replaced

     d. The amount of insurance stated in the policy

4. The Conditions section also specifies that insured property may have unscheduled coverage by which articles are covered on a blanket basis, such as stamps in a collection, subject to an absolute dollar amount (such as $250 per any one stamp).

C. Coverages in the ISO inland marine program can be specialized, with forms covering a single category of personal property, or general, with forms that are broader and generic in nature. Three general forms are commonly used:

1. The Personal Articles Standard Loss Settlement Form provides special form coverage for several classes of personal property, including jewelry and musical instruments.

     a. It excludes losses caused by wear and tear, deterioration, inherent vice, or insects or vermin.

     b. Additional exclusions apply to fine arts.

2. The Personal Property Form provides special form coverage on unscheduled personal property owned or used by the insured and normally kept at the insured's residence.

     a. It also provides worldwide coverage on the same property when it is temporarily away from the residence premises.

     b. Separate amounts of insurance are provided for thirteen classes of unscheduled property.

3. The Personal Effects Form provides special form coverage on personal property such as luggage, clothes, cameras, and sports equipment normally worn or carried by tourists and travelers. Property is covered worldwide, but only while it is away from the insured's permanent residence. These types of property are excluded:

     a. Account, bills, currency, deeds, securities, passports

b. Animals

c. Artificial teeth or limbs

d. Contact lenses

e. Bicycles, hovercraft, motors, motor vehicles, watercraft

f. Household furniture

g. Merchandise for sale or exhibition

h. Physicians' and surgeons' instruments

i. Salesperson's samples

j. Theatrical property

k. Contraband property in the course of illegal transport or trade

---

Educational Objective 2

Compare the coverages typically provided for watercraft under each of the following:

- **HO-3**

- **Personal Auto Policy**

- **Small boat policies**

- **Boatowners and yacht policies**

Key Points:

Personal watercraft insurance is available to meet the watercraft coverage needs of individuals and families. Personal watercraft includes small rowboats, canoes, outboard and inboard motorboats, sailboats, houseboats, and power yachts.

A. HO-3 watercraft coverage provides property and liability coverage for watercraft and related equipment.

   1. Homeowners Section I—Property Coverages provides limited physical damage coverage that may be adequate for rowboats, canoes, and small outboard boats.

      a. A $1,500 limit applies to watercraft, including trailers, furnishings, and equipment.

      b. Coverage is provided on a named-perils-only basis.

      c. Windstorm coverage applies (up to the $1,500 limit) only when the craft is inside a fully enclosed building.

      d. Theft coverage does not apply to the boat and motor when away from the residence premises; accessories, trailers, and other boating personal property are excluded from this coverage.

   2. Homeowners Section II—Liability Coverages includes a detailed watercraft exclusion focusing on craft of certain size and length. Section II covers only certain limited watercraft loss exposures:

      a. All watercraft not powered, except sailing vessels twenty-six feet or more in length.

      b. All inboard, inboard-outdrive, and sailing vessels not owned or rented by an insured. Therefore, any boat borrowed or operated on behalf of an insured is covered.

      c. All inboard and inboard-outdrive boats of fifty horsepower or less, rented to an insured.

    d. All sailing vessels with auxiliary power, if less than twenty-six feet long.

    e. All boats powered by an outboard motor or motors, unless the motor both exceeds twenty-five horsepower and was owned by an insured at policy inception.

B. Personal Auto Policy watercraft coverage does not provide physical damage or liability coverage for watercraft, motors, or watercraft-related equipment.

    1. However, physical damage loss is covered for a boat trailer described on the PAP Declarations page.

    2. The PAP also covers nonowned trailers under Part D—Coverage for Damage to Your Auto to a limit of $1,500.

C. Small boat policies are designed to provide more comprehensive coverage for boats up to a certain size (such as twenty-six feet in length). Although small boat policies are not standard, they have certain common features:

    1. Covered property—A small boat policy may cover the boat, motor, equipment, and trailer. Most small boat policies are written on an actual cash value basis and contain a deductible, such as $100, $250, or more.

    2. Covered perils—A small boat policy can be written to provide named perils or special form ("all-risks") coverage.

        a. Most small boat policies are of the special form type and cover all direct physical losses to covered watercraft except those excluded.

        b. Generally, a small boat policy includes liability insurance for bodily injury, loss of life, illness, and property damage to third parties arising out of the ownership, maintenance, or use of the boat.

        c. Medical payments coverage is typically included for any insured person who sustains bodily injury while in, upon, boarding, or leaving the boat.

    3. These major exclusions are commonly found in small boat policies:

        a. General risks of direct loss—Excludes coverage for loss caused by wear and tear, gradual deterioration, vermin and marine life, rust and corrosion, inherent vice, latent defect, mechanical breakdown, or extremes of temperature.

        b. Repair or service—Excludes coverage for loss or damage from refinishing, renovating, or repair.

    c. Business pursuits—Excludes coverage if the boat is used to carry passengers for compensation, if the boat or insured property is rented to others, or if the covered property is being operated in any official race or speed contest.

D. Boatowners and yacht policies provide coverage for larger boats that are not covered under small boat policies. Boatowners and yacht policies contain certain common features:

  1. Warranties—Personal watercraft insurance generally contains several warranties. If a warranty is violated, higher premiums may be required, or the coverages may not apply, depending on the warranty. These are the major personal watercraft insurance warranties:

    a. Pleasure use—The insured warrants that the boat will be used only for private, pleasure purposes and will not be hired or chartered unless the insurer approves.

    b. Seaworthiness—The insured warrants that the boat is in a seaworthy condition.

    c. Lay-up period—The insured warrants that the boat will not be in operation during certain periods, such as during the winter months. The lay-up period is usually shown on the Declarations page.

    d. Navigational limits—These warranties, stated on the policy's Declarations page, limit the use of the vessel to a certain geographical area.

  2. Persons insured—The insured includes those named on the Declarations page, resident relatives of the household, and persons under the age of twenty-one in the insured's care. The insured's paid captain and crew are also considered insureds. Other persons or organizations using the boat without a charge are covered provided the named insured gives permission.

  3. Physical damage coverage—Boatowners and yacht policies contain physical damage coverage on either a named perils or a special form basis covering the boat or "hull," equipment, accessories, motor, and trailer. Certain property damage exclusions are commonly found in these policies:

    a. Wear and tear, gradual deterioration, rust, corrosion, mold, wet or dry rot, marring, denting, scratching, inherent vice, latent or physical defect, insects, animal or marine life, weathering, and dampness of atmosphere.

    b. Mechanical breakdown or faulty manufacturing, unless the loss was caused by fire or explosion.

    c. Freezing and thawing of ice, unless the insured has taken reasonable care to protect the property.

    d. Loss that occurs while the boat is used in any official race or speed contest. Most watercraft policies do not exclude sailboat racing.

    e. Intentional loss caused by an insured.

    f. War, nuclear hazard, and radioactive contamination.

4. Liability coverage—In addition to covering bodily injury and property damage perils related to the operation of watercraft, boatowners and yacht policies typically include a form of liability coverage called protection and indemnity (P&I) insurance. Certain liability exclusions are commonly found in boatowners and yacht policies:

    a. Intentional injury or illegal activities

    b. Renting the watercraft to others or carrying persons or property for a fee without the insurer's permission

    c. Liability arising out of water-skiing, parasailing, or other airborne or experimental devices

    d. Using watercraft (except sailboats in some policies) in any official race or speed test

    e. Losses covered by a workers compensation or similar law

    f. Bodily injury or property damage arising out of transportation of the boat on land

    g. Liability assumed under a contract

    h. Injury to an employee if the employee's work involves operation or maintenance of the watercraft

    i. Business use

    j. Discharge or escape of pollutants unless sudden or accidental

    k. War, insurrection, rebellion, and nuclear perils

5. Medical payments coverage under boatowners and yacht policies includes coverage for such bodily-injury related expenses as medical, surgical, X-ray, dental, ambulance, hospital, professional nursing, and funeral services; and for first aid rendered at the time of the accident.

6. Other coverages—Additional coverages may added to or provided in boatowners and yacht policies:

    a. Uninsured boaters coverage, by endorsement or as a coverage option

    b. The insured's liability for injury to maritime workers (except crew members) injured in the course of employment

    c. The legal obligation of the insured to remove a wrecked or sunken vessel following a loss

    d. Bodily injury or property damage arising out of transportation of the boat on land, for an additional premium

    e. Damage to or loss of the insured's personal effects, for a limited amount

    f. The cost of commercial towing and assistance, for a limited amount

    g. Hurricane protection coverage, by endorsement, to reimburse boatowners for the costs of removing their watercraft from the water or moving the boat to a safe harbor because of an approaching storm

Educational Objective 3
Summarize the coverage provided by the typical personal umbrella policy.

Key Points:

Most personal umbrella policies provide not only higher limits but also broader coverage than underlying personal insurance policies. A personal umbrella policy provides liability protection to insureds for amounts over the liability limits on existing homeowners, personal auto, and watercraft policies.

A. A personal umbrella policy is designed to provide bodily injury, personal injury, and property damage liability coverage in case of a catastrophic claim, lawsuit, or judgment.

  1. Umbrella coverage provides additional liability limits over any underlying insurance policies, such as Homeowners Section II—Liability Coverages, personal auto liability, and personal watercraft liability policies.

  2. The personal umbrella policy also typically provides drop-down coverage, which is broader than the underlying coverage. When underlying insurance does not apply to a particular loss and the loss is not excluded by the umbrella coverage, the umbrella coverage "drops down" to cover the entire loss, less a self-insured retention of between $250 and $10,000.

  3. The amount of personal umbrella coverage purchased typically ranges from $1 million to $10 million.

  4. The policy covers the named insured, resident relatives, and usually persons using (with the insured's permission) cars, motorcycles, recreational vehicles, or any watercraft owned by or rented to the named insured.

B. Most insurers' umbrella policies contain these provisions:

  1. Insuring Agreement—This provision covers bodily injury and property damage, as well as personal injury for which an insured becomes legally liable.

   a. It includes coverage for legal defense costs that are not payable by the underlying insurance policies.

   b. Some states require the insurer to offer the insured the option to extend the personal umbrella to cover uninsured and underinsured motorists protection.

2. Exclusions—Because personal umbrella policies provide broad coverage, certain important exclusions usually are included:
   a. Intentional injury
   b. Business property and pursuits
   c. Professional liability
   d. Aircraft
   e. Watercraft
   f. Recreational vehicles
   g. Transmission of any communicable diseases
   h. Directors and officers
   i. Damage to insured's property
   j. Workers compensation
   k. Nuclear energy
3. Conditions—These are some of the important conditions in the personal umbrella policy:
   a. The insured must maintain the underlying insurance coverages and limits shown in the declarations.
   b. The insured must give the insurer written notice of loss as soon as practicable.
   c. The umbrella policy is excess over any other insurance, whether collectible or not.
   d. The policy territory is worldwide.

Educational Objective 4

Given a case describing a liability claim, determine:

- **Whether the loss would be covered by a personal umbrella policy**

- **The dollar amount, if any, payable under the umbrella policy**

- **The dollar amount, if any, payable under the underlying insurance policies**

- **The dollar amount, if any, payable by the insured**

Key Points:

To adequately meet the requirements of this case study's Educational Objective, students should understand the DICE method of policy analysis as well as the specific policy forms and endorsements described in the case to make accurate coverage and loss settlement amount determinations.

To determine whether a policy covers a loss, many insurance professionals apply the DICE method. ("DICE" is an acronym for categories of policy provisions: declarations, insuring agreement, conditions, and exclusions.) The DICE method has four steps:

1. Review of the declarations page to determine whether it covers the person or the property at the time of the loss

2. Review of the insuring agreement to determine whether it covers the loss

3. Review of policy conditions to determine compliance

4. Review of policy exclusions to determine whether they preclude coverage of the loss

Each of these four steps is used in every case. Other categories of policy provisions should be examined. For example, endorsements and terms defined in the policy should be reviewed in relation to the declarations, insuring agreement, exclusions, and conditions.

Key Words and Phrases:

Key Words

Inland marine insurance
Insurance that covers many different classes of property that typically involve an element of transportation.

Residence premises
The place where the insured resides as identified in the policy declarations.

Blanket basis
A basis for insuring all items within a single amount of insurance without specifically identifying each item.

Personal effects
Personal property items owned by individuals that are personal in nature, such as jewelry, clothes, wallets, or purses.

Perils of the sea
Accidental causes of loss that are peculiar to the sea and other bodies of water.

Warranty
A promise made by an insured that guarantees compliance with the insurer's conditions.

Hull insurance
Insurance that covers physical damage to vessels, including their machinery and fuel but not their cargo.

Protection and indemnity (P&I) insurance
Insurance that covers shipowners against various liability claims due to operating the insured vessel.

Uninsured boaters coverage
Coverage for the insured's bodily injury incurred in a boating accident caused by another boat's owner or operator who is uninsured and who is legally responsible for the injury; similar to the PAP's uninsured motorists coverage.

United States Longshore and Harbor Workers' Compensation Act Endorsement
An endorsement that amends the Workers Compensation and Employers Liability Insurance Policy to cover the insured's obligations under the U.S. Longshore and Harbor Workers Compensation Act.

Life Insurance Planning

10

Key Points:

Life insurance is a means by which individuals and families can reduce or eliminate the financial impact of the premature death loss exposure. Several types of individuals and families can benefit from having life insurance.

Study Tips

The review questions help reinforce this material. Take some time now to complete them.

A. Costs Associated With Premature Death

   1. The costs required to support one's family over a lifetime are significant and can vary depending on the specific type of family structure.

   2. When a family's key wage earner dies prematurely, replacement income is not always readily available.

   3. Life insurance is a key financial planning tool that is often used to provide for these costs associated with premature death:

      a. Lost income

      Deceased wage earner's income is lost.

      b. Final costs

      Funeral costs, medical expenses, and so forth.

      c. Outstanding debts

      Credit card debts, mortgage, and so forth.

    d. Unpaid long-term obligations

To supplement retirement savings and fund college tuitions, child care expenses, home maintenance expenses, and so forth.

    e. Estate planning costs

Estate taxes, probate costs, lost charitable contributions, and so forth.

    f. Unfulfilled family obligations

Both economic and noneconomic; for example, the family's standard of living may be adversely affected or a child may grieve over the loss of a parent.

B. Singles Without Children

    1. Singles without children are individuals who are not married or in a long-term, committed relationship and who do not have dependent children.

    2. A single person may not need life insurance to reduce the financial impact of the premature death loss exposure if no one financially depends on him or her; just a small amount of life insurance may be required to cover funeral expenses and any uninsured medical expenses.

    3. Singles may want life insurance to provide financial support for elderly parents or other family members, cover any significant debt that might pass on to surviving family members, or allocate toward any estate taxes payable or to fund gifts or trusts for designated survivors.

C. Single-Parent Families

    1. Singles with children include single parents, single grandparents caring for a child, or other relatives or guardians who fulfill parental responsibilities related to a dependent child or children.

    2. The financial impact of the loss of a single person with a child or children can be significant.

    3. Frequently, singles with children have little or no life insurance, relying instead on government insurance resources such as Social Security survivors benefits.

    4. Singles with children can use life insurance as a tool to ensure that their loved ones will be cared for properly in terms of housing, education, and other expenses, and they can use the process of obtaining life insurance (which can include drafting a will) to appoint guardians of their choice for their dependent children.

D. Two-Income Families With Children

    1. Two-income families with children can include unmarried couples (including relatives or guardians) who care for dependent children. However, this category is primarily populated with individuals who are married and employed and who have children.

    2. The loss of one spouse's earnings can affect the surviving spouse's ability to properly maintain the household, provide for related expenses, fund future retirement, and ensure the financial well-being of the children beyond any governmental benefits they may receive.

    3. Life insurance can enable the family to maintain its "two-income" standard of living.

E. Two-Income Families Without Children

    1. Two-income families without children can include individuals who are married or are in a long-term, committed relationship but who do not care for dependent children.

    2. The premature death of one wage earner can leave the surviving wage earner facing financial implications that modest amounts of life insurance can address, such as satisfying outstanding indebtedness, supporting aging parents or other financially dependent relatives, making mortgage payments, supplying funds for retirement, or maintaining his or her current lifestyle.

F. "Traditional" Families

    1. In the traditional family category, only one parent is employed, while the other partner manages the household and takes care of the dependent children.

    2. The number of traditional families has declined in recent years because of economic pressures and changing lifestyles.

    3. The premature death of the working spouse can leave the surviving spouse with household expenses that must still be met, mortgages to be paid, retirement to be funded, and allocations to be provided for children's education costs.

        a. The surviving spouse may need to return to the workforce, thus possibly generating child-care costs.

        b. Life insurance benefits, in addition to Social Security survivors benefits, can greatly mitigate this significant uncertainty.

    4. If the deceased parent was the spouse managing the household and taking care of dependent children, the death of that individual can have a financial impact because the household must still be maintained and managed and child-care costs may be incurred or may increase.

G. Blended Families

1. A blended family is a family unit in which one or both partners bring with them dependent children from a prior relationship. One or both partners in the blended family may be employed.

2. Unique financial needs of the blended family relate to the dependent children; children from a previous relationship may be older and reaching the ages at which education costs and the costs of supporting them escalate. Children may be born into the blended relationship, extending the timeline for child-care costs.

3. Life insurance can offset the uncertainty of such expenses, particularly when other contractual resources for these expenses, such as alimony and child support, may be limited.

H. "Sandwiched" Families

1. A typical sandwiched family could consist of an aging parent or dependent family member who receives financial assistance or other types of support from his or her adult child or another younger relative. This same adult child or younger relative, in turn, supports his or her own dependent children.

2. The premature death of a wage earner can dramatically reduce the funds available to support not only dependent children but also dependent aging parents or other relatives. Funds may no longer be available to help maintain the current standard of living or manage the household.

3. Death of a nonworking member of the sandwiched generation can generate an increase in child-care costs and also other costs related to the nonfinancial support (such as physical care) and support of aging parents or other dependent relatives.

4. Life insurance can be used to offset these increased costs as well as to fund retirement income; a deceased working spouse can no longer contribute to any retirement programs.

Educational Objective 2

Describe the needs approach and the human life value approach for determining the appropriate amount of life insurance.

Key Points:

Several methods exist for estimating the amount of life insurance an individual requires in order to reduce or eliminate the financial uncertainty of a premature death. Two basic methods are precise ways to estimate life insurance amounts.

A. Needs Approach

The needs approach is used to identify an adequate amount of life insurance based on survivors' needs, including those of the decedent's family or other dependents. A needs and benefits/assets review typically generates results that fall into one or more of these financial categories:

1. Final expenses needs

Incurred immediately before death and immediately thereafter, these expenses can include a decedent's uninsured medical bills, funeral and burial costs, federal estate taxes and state inheritance (estate) taxes, and any probate costs.

2. Debt elimination needs

Debt elimination relates to a decedent's outstanding debt or financial obligations.

3. Family living expense needs

A family's living expenses include any expense required to maintain the household, provide for child care, or fund any other expenses related to daily living.

   a. When determining the family's living expenses, consideration is given to any income that might be generated by a surviving spouse.

   b. Financial requirements that exceed the surviving spouse's income are calculated per year and multiplied by the projected total number of years of need.

4. Special needs

These are expenses that remain or financial obligations that must be funded after an individual's death, and include monetary gifts, a trust, or an emergency fund.

5. Retirement income needs

   A needs and benefits/assets review should consider the impact of a premature death on sources of retirement benefits other than the Social Security benefits the survivor will receive when he or she becomes eligible for them.

6. Life insurance and other assets

   Existing life insurance and any other income-producing assets that can be used to fund survivors' well-being and to help them maintain their previous standard of living are totaled and applied to their financial requirements to determine an appropriate amount of life insurance.

B. Human Life Value Approach

1. The human life value approach estimates an individual's income for his or her remaining working life and factors in other items such as the individual's age in relation to retirement and the cost of self-maintenance.

   a. Cost of self-maintenance means that portion of total wages that the wage earner consumes in the course of daily living.

   b. The surplus amount is the remaining wages that go to the family to meet its needs. This surplus is the human life value.

2. A present value factor is applied to the total amount of income requiring replacement—the human life value.

3. A separate calculation is made to estimate the total of any existing life insurance, savings and investments, and Social Security benefits.

   a. A present value factor is applied to any additional income item that is received over time, such as Social Security benefits.

   b. This sum is then subtracted from the human life value to determine the total amount of new or additional life insurance required.

4. This approach, which focuses on replacing a primary wage earner's lost income, typically develops a lower appropriate insurance amount than does the needs approach.

Educational Objective 3
Summarize the various types of life insurance.

Key Points:

Common types of life insurance that meet the needs of most insureds include these:

A. Term Life

1. Term insurance is life insurance that provides coverage for a specified period, such as ten or twenty years, with no cash value. If the insured dies during the policy term, the policy value is paid to the beneficiary.

2. Term insurance is regarded as temporary protection.

3. It is life insurance only; it has no savings, investment, or cash value/loan value aspect.

4. Term life is useful to someone whose current need for life insurance will diminish after a number of years.

5. Term is often a low-cost way to obtain life insurance to protect income during critical times.

    a. For some term policies, premiums increase with the insured's age and are based on mortality rates. Because mortality rates increase with age, term insurance premiums also increase.

    b. A popular form of term (level term) has a fixed annual premium for a fixed number of years. Insureds with level term pay a higher rate in the early years in exchange for a flat, affordable rate in the later years of the term.

6. Most term policies carry some guarantee of renewability, so that the insured can continue the insurance beyond a fixed number of years (although doing so may require a higher rate).

    a. Insurers typically do not allow renewal after a certain age, such as sixty-five, seventy, or seventy-five.

    b. Some insurers guarantee renewability to an older age, such as ninety-five or ninety-nine.

7. Many policies are also convertible, so that the insured may exchange the term policy for a whole life policy without meeting any new insurability requirements such as a physical examination.

B. Whole Life

1. Whole life insurance is a hybrid combination of life insurance and an investment vehicle.

2. Its coverage is not limited to a fixed period and it is designed to provide coverage for a lifetime.

3. For a given amount of coverage, the annual premium for whole life is higher than for term life. The selling point is that whole life is a savings vehicle that develops a cash value as time passes.

4. In the early years of a whole life policy, insureds pay an annual premium that covers more than the projected mortality costs for insureds at that age.

   a. In effect, the extra money is used to build the cash value.

   b. The cash value is available to the insured during the life of the policy, either as a loan or as a cash payment upon surrender of the policy.

C. Universal Life

1. Like whole life, universal life is a permanent product that combines life insurance protection with an investment or a savings aspect.

2. The insured makes premium payments that exceed the amount needed to cover the mortality risk (cost of insurance). The policyholder accumulates cash value from the amount of premiums paid in excess of the cost of the insurance protection and expenses.

3. The unbundling of the insurance protection, savings, and expense components is the distinguishing characteristic of universal life. Policyholders receive an annual disclosure that shows the amount of premiums paid, the amount of insurance (death benefit), expenses, and interest earned and credited on the cash value.

4. Another hallmark of universal life is that two interest rates are stipulated in the policy.

   a. One is a guaranteed minimum rate that the cash value of the policy is guaranteed to earn interest at.

   b. The other rate is the current market interest rate; if that rate is higher than the guaranteed minimum rate, the cash value will earn that higher rate.

5. For most universal life policies, the insured's premium payments are flexible, provided that there is enough cash value in the policy to cover the cost of insurance and expenses. If the insured pays higher premiums, growth in cash value is tax-deferred.

6. The insured has options to increase the death benefit, borrow against the cash value, withdraw from (and thereby reduce) the cash value, or add insureds to the policy.

7. The flexibility allows insureds to be less than fully committed to a premium payment discipline, and policies can lapse when premiums are not paid and the cash value is insufficient to cover the cost of insurance and expenses.

8. In an environment of falling rates, the cash value may grow more slowly than hoped and require larger premium payments to maintain the coverage.

D. Variable Life

1. This policy provides cash value over time and permanent insurance protection, but it enables policyholders to choose among investment accounts offered by the insurer and to move cash values among these accounts.

2. The investment performance results of the accounts affect the amount of the policy cash values and sometimes the death benefit.

3. Variable life insurance offers level premiums and is appropriate for persons who want the benefit of using competitive investment strategies and some protection against inflation over the life of their insurance program. The policy should be held for several years, such as five, ten, fifteen, or twenty, to take full advantage of the flexible investment benefit.

4. A significant advantage is that the policyholder can move the policy cash value amount among investments without incurring any current income tax liability for capital gains.

E. Variable Universal Life

1. This combines the features of universal life insurance and variable life insurance.

2. The cash values in variable universal life insurance are not guaranteed, nor is any minimum interest rate. The cash value of the policy is determined by the investment experience of a separate account that is maintained by the insurer.

3. The policyholder can select the separate account in which the flexible premiums are invested.

4. Insurers impose significant initial expense charges and sometimes surrender charges (based on potential sales charges) for managing policyholder investment accounts. The latter charges decline after the policy ages ten to fifteen years and usually reaches zero.

5. Insurers may charge annual (or periodic) investment management fees, expense charges, and sometimes other administration fees.

6. Insurers charge for the mortality cost of insurance protection provided by the policy.

F. Other Types of Life Insurance

1. Current assumption whole life

   a. This insurance (also called interest-sensitive life insurance) includes features of a traditional whole life policy and a universal life policy.

   b. The premium and the cash value can be periodically recalculated by the insurer, based on new actuarial assumptions (drawn from the insurer's investment results and loss experience).

   c. The insurer guarantees a minimum interest rate, and some insurers offer maximum mortality and expense charges.

2. Second-to-die (survivorship) life insurance

   a. In this policy, two lives are insured in a single policy, with death benefits payable to the beneficiary when both insureds have died.

   b. These survivorship policies can be traditional fixed-premium whole life policies, current assumption policies, universal life, or even a combination of permanent and term life insurance.

   c. Premiums for such policies are typically lower than those of a comparable policy on an individual life because benefits are not payable until both lives have ended.

3. First-to-die (joint) life insurance

   a. These policies cover two individuals and the death benefit is payable upon the first death.

   b. The appeal of such a policy is that when the first person dies, the death benefit can provide the survivor with funds to cover a home mortgage, other personal or business debt obligations, and dependent care.

   c. Although premiums are typically higher than for second-to-die policies, this option is less costly than taking separate policies on each life.

Educational Objective 4

Summarize the distinguishing characteristics of life insurance provided by each of the following sources: individual life insurance, group life insurance, government-provided life insurance.

Key Points:

Individuals need life insurance to protect those who depend on their income or services. Although people frequently purchase individual life insurance policies, coverage can also be obtained in group life insurance plans and government-sponsored plans.

A. Individually Purchased Life Insurance

When consumers select and buy their own policies, their choices are maximized. The life insurance marketplace offers a wide variety of products, such as term life insurance, whole life insurance, universal life insurance, and variable life insurance.

1. Advantages of individual life insurance

   a. Consumers who obtain their own life insurance coverage have maximum control.

   - The insurance would not be subject to the kinds of changes that might be made to the coverage in an employer-sponsored group life insurance plan.

   - There is no threat that coverage would end due to retirement or other termination of employment.

   b. The buyer of individual life insurance has more choices of types and terms of life insurance.

   c. For some insured employees, particularly younger persons, the cost of individual life insurance may be less than the price of group term insurance.

   d. Individual life insurance can be sold by a life insurance agent who can render professional service to the policyholder.

2. Limitations of individual life insurance

   a. For most workers, the cost of individual life insurance is probably greater than that of comparable group insurance because of the lower administrative costs for group coverage and the employer's contribution to the cost.

   b. Its purchase is less convenient than receiving group coverage or government coverage.

   c. Individual life insurance offers no tax advantages to purchasers; the premium for individual coverage is paid with after-tax dollars.

    d. Since individual life insurance is individually underwritten by the insurer, persons in ill health or otherwise regarded as high-risk applicants may have difficulty securing affordable coverage, or coverage at any price.

B. Group Life Insurance

Group life insurance provides coverage to a number of individuals under one master contract issued to a sponsoring organization. Plans can be financed solely by employers (noncontributory plans) or might require contributions from employees (contributory plans). To guard against adverse selection, insurers typically require 100 percent participation for noncontributory plans and that a certain percentage (generally about 75 percent) of eligible employees participate for contributory plans.

   1. Group selection

    a. Group insurance is generally provided without a medical examination or other evidence of insurability.

    b. Characteristics of the group as a whole—such as turnover rates, industry, stability of the group members, and average age—are underwritten. If a group is acceptable, then generally all members of the group are eligible for coverage.

   2. Eligible employees or members

    a. Generally, group insurance protects all regular, full-time employees (or members) of an organization. Many plans have a probationary-period requirement.

    b. According to state laws and most insurer underwriting rules, an employer can establish standards to cover only certain classes of employees, but the standard cannot exclude individuals based on age, sex, race, or religion.

   3. Benefits

    a. The amount of life insurance may be determined automatically, through a formula or schedule, to minimize adverse selection.

    b. In some plans (known as flexible benefits or cafeteria-style plans), employees can choose from among a number of kinds and amounts of employee benefits. Employees who select group life insurance over certain amounts usually must show individual evidence of insurability.

    c. Popular practice is to provide life insurance equal to some multiple of the employee's annual salary, often one, two, or three times rounded to the nearest $1,000. Many insurers stipulate a minimum and maximum amount.

4. Typical coverage
   a. The majority of employer-sponsored group life insurance is yearly renewable term insurance.
      • This coverage is pure protection and does not develop a cash value.
      • Yearly renewable term protection expires at the end of each policy year but is automatically renewed.
      • The premium charged to the employer usually changes annually to reflect the experience of the group being insured.
      • The employer often pays all or part of the premium, but it is common for employees to contribute to the cost, especially at higher amounts of coverage.
   b. The cost of the group life, if paid by the employer, can be considered as income to an employee covered in a group life plan.
   c. The Internal Revenue Service (IRS) allows employees to exclude, from their gross wages, the premiums for the first $50,000 of coverage paid by the employer on their behalf to purchase the group term life insurance.

5. Advantages of group life insurance

   For employer-sponsored group life plans, yearly renewable term is popular for these reasons:
   a. Low premiums, as compared to whole life plans
   b. Simplicity of administration
   c. Income tax advantages
   d. Convenience of payroll deduction (to the extent that employee contributes)
   e. Lack of requirement of proof of insurability

6. Limitations of group life insurance
   a. Depending on company underwriting practices and the benefit schedule, an individual may not be able to obtain more than a modest amount of protection.
   b. A benefit schedule might provide less coverage to younger, lower-paid employees.
   c. Typically, group life coverage is continued for an employee for only thirty-one days following termination.
   d. Many group life plans offer no post-retirement coverage options or only a small percentage of the coverage that was in effect during employment.
   e. Group life is sold on a mass production basis, and employees may not receive expert advice.

C. Government-Provided Life Insurance

Life insurance coverage is also provided as part of Social Security. Benefits accrue during an individual's years of employment. Social Security benefits include monthly death benefits for surviving spouses and other family members:

1. Surviving spouses

    a. Widows or widowers of an individual eligible to receive Social Security benefits can receive full benefits when they reach retirement age.

- This age varies based on the survivor's date of birth but is generally over the age of sixty-six.
- Reduced benefits are paid to surviving spouses starting at age sixty.
- If a surviving spouse is disabled, benefits may start as early as age fifty.

    b. Divorced spouses are also eligible for survivors benefits if the marriage lasted for ten years or longer.

    c. Surviving spouses of any age who are caring for dependent children younger than sixteen years are also eligible for reduced benefits, generally 75 percent of the decedent's benefits.

2. Dependent children and parents

    a. Unmarried children are also eligible to receive Social Security survivors benefits if they are less than eighteen years of age. Benefits will be paid up to age nineteen if the child is attending school full time.

    b. Benefits are also payable to disabled surviving children if the disability occurred before the age of twenty-two.

    c. Parents who are dependent on the deceased individual can receive survivors benefits.

- For parents to be considered dependent, they must have relied on the decedent for at least half of their living support.
- Dependent parents must be at least sixty-two years old to receive dependent parent benefits.

Educational Objective 5
Summarize the common life insurance contractual provisions and riders.

Key Points:

Life insurance policies contain several common contractual provisions that apply to the coverage and benefits provided. Riders that provide optional benefits are also available.

A. Common Life Insurance Contractual Provisions

  1. Assignment clause

  a. A life insurance policyowner can assign the policy to another person.

  b. An absolute assignment transfers all ownership rights to another party.

  c. A collateral assignment assigns the policy to another as collateral for a loan. A collateral assignment transfers only certain policy rights to a creditor.

  2. Beneficiary designations

  a. Most policies indicate a primary beneficiary, who will be the first to collect benefits under the policy.

  b. Some policies name a contingent beneficiary to receive benefits if the primary beneficiary is not alive at the time of the insured's death.

  c. A revocable beneficiary designation denotes that the policyowner can make beneficiary changes without the beneficiary's consent.

  d. An irrevocable beneficiary designation means beneficiary changes must have the beneficiary's consent.

  e. Beneficiary designations can be specific or designated as a class.

  3. Dividend options

  a. Life insurance policies that pay dividends are called participating policies.

  b. An insurer may pay dividends based on its favorable loss, expenses, or investment results. Dividends, however, are not guaranteed.

   c. Several dividend options are available under a participating life insurance policy:
- Cash option
  Dividends are paid in cash, usually at the policy anniversary date.
- Accumulated option
  Dividend amounts remain with the insurer and accumulate interest. Dividends and accumulated interest can subsequently be withdrawn at any time or can be left to be paid in addition to death benefit amounts.
- Premium reduction option
  Dividend amounts can be applied to pay for future premium payments due.
- Paid-up additions
  Dividends may be used to buy increments of paid-up whole life insurance, which increases the amount of the death benefit paid under the policy.
- One-year term insurance
  Dividends may also be used to purchase term, rather than whole, life insurance for one year. If the insured dies within that time, the term life amount is added to the death benefit payable under the policy.

4. Excluded risks

   a. Some life insurance policies specify types of losses that are not covered.

   b. Such exclusions usually involve hazardous occupations or recreational activities of the insured.

   c. Some life insurance policies exclude coverage for death during active military service or while in an aircraft other than a commercial airliner.

5. Grace period

   a. The grace period provides the policyowner additional time to pay overdue life insurance premiums.

   b. For most policies, the grace period is thirty-one days.

   c. If an insured dies during the grace period, death benefits would still be paid. Generally, the death benefit is reduced by the overdue premium amount.

6. Incontestable clause

The incontestable clause designates a period, usually two years, after which the insurer cannot deny a claim because of any misrepresentation on the part of the policyowner.

7. Misstatement of age or sex

    a. The misstatement of age or sex provision allows the insurer to adjust the death benefit on a life insurance policy to reflect the true age and sex of the insured based on the amount of the premium paid.

    b. A misstatement of sex is also treated by adjusting the face amount of the policy (when different premiums apply for males and females).

8. Nonforfieture options

    a. Because life insurance policies accumulate cash value, all states have enacted nonforfeiture laws to protect the financial interests of policyowners who terminate their policies.

    b. These laws require insurers to pay a portion of the policy's cash value if the policyowner terminates the policy.

    c. Policyowners have three nonforfeiture options:

        • Cash surrender value

        The policyowner would surrender the policy for cash and all of the insurer's future obligations under the policy would cease. Any outstanding loan amounts would be deducted from the cash surrender amount. Cash surrender amounts are determined based on nonforfeiture tables.

        • Reduced paid-up insurance

        The policyowner may elect to use the accumulated cash value in the policy to purchase paid-up insurance at a reduced face amount. The type of coverage provided is the same as that provided under the original contract that was surrendered.

        • Extended term insurance

        The policyowner may choose to continue the full death benefit of the original policy, but for a shorter period, under a term policy.

9. Policy loan provisions

    a. Life insurance policies that accumulate cash value contain a policy loan provision.

    b. Under this provision, policyowners can borrow an amount up to the cash value of the policy.

    c. Policy loans are subject to interest, which is generally stated in the contract.

    d. If a policy loan is not paid at the time of the insured's death, outstanding loan amounts (including interest) are deducted from the death benefit amount.

    e. Because no repayment schedule is set for life insurance policy loans, the policyowner has flexibility in repaying the loan.

10. Reinstatement clause

    a. The reinstatement clause allows a policyowner to reinstate a life insurance policy that has lapsed for nonpayment of premium.

    b. Most insurers allow reinstatement within a specified period, such as three or five years after the policy has lapsed.

11. Settlement option

Death benefits under a life insurance policy can be paid to the beneficiary in a single lump sum. The policyowner or beneficiary, however, has additional settlement options available:

    a. Interest option

- The life insurer retains the death benefits and pays only the interest to the beneficiary at periodic intervals.
- This option is generally used on an interim basis until the lump-sum payment or another settlement option is made.

    b. Fixed-period option

- The death benefits are paid over a specified period of time.
- This option is appropriate when it is possible to determine how long income will be needed.

    c. Fixed-amount options

- Death benefits are paid in fixed amounts at predetermined intervals, usually monthly. Interest payments are included in the fixed amount.
- In most cases, the beneficiary can be provided with a limited or unlimited right to withdraw the proceeds, change the benefit amount, and select an alternative settlement option for the unpaid proceeds.

    d. Life income option

- The beneficiary receives the death benefit over his or her life.
- Life income options may include a no-refund option, which will pay benefits only until the death of the beneficiary. Other life income options would allow for payments remaining after the primary beneficiary's death to be paid to a contingent beneficiary.

12. Suicide clause

    a. All life insurance policies contain a suicide clause that excludes coverage for suicide of the insured, while sane or insane, within two years from the date of policy issue.

    b. Most policies will refund the policy premium to the beneficiary if a suicide occurs in the first two years of the policy.

B. Common Life Insurance Riders

Additional premiums are generally charged for these coverage extensions:

1. Accelerated death benefits

    a. In the case of a catastrophic or terminal illness, the insured may need to access life insurance benefits to finance medical expenses before death.

    b. Some life insurers offer riders that provide for the discounted value, or a portion of such value, of the policy death benefit to be paid to the policyowner in the event of certain contingencies, such as a terminal illness.

    c. Other riders may cover a catastrophic illness, or the need for long-term care in a nursing home or similar facility.

2. Accidental death benefits

    a. This benefit (often referred to as "double indemnity") provides an additional death benefit when death results from accidental bodily injury or accidental means as defined in the rider.

    b. In most cases, the amount of the accidental death benefit is equal to the face amount of the basic policy—in other words, it doubles the amount payable for accidental death.

    c. Some insurers automatically include this benefit in the policy and do not require a separate premium.

3. Disability income rider

This rider may be added to a life insurance policy to provide a regular monthly income if the insured becomes permanently disabled.

4. Guaranteed insurability rider

    a. This rider provides the policyowner the option to purchase additional life insurance at specified times in the future without evidence of insurability.

    b. This option must normally be purchased before a certain age, often forty. The option dates are usually set at uniform intervals based on the insured's attained age.

    c. The type of insurance that can be purchased under this option is usually limited to a form of whole life insurance.

    d. A minimum amount often applies to the exercise of this option, and the maximum amount of insurance that can be purchased is often limited to the death benefit on the original policy or some specified maximum portion of that death benefit.

5. Waiver of premium rider
   a. The insurer agrees to waive the payment of any premium falling due while the policyowner or insured is disabled as defined in the waiver of premium provision.
   b. The provisions, values, and benefits of the basic policy will be the same during the time of the disability as if the premium payments had actually been made to the insurer.
   c. To be eligible for the benefit, the policyowner must have incurred a disability before the age stipulated in the contract.

Educational Objective 6

Given a scenario regarding a particular family structure with its associated financial and family obligations, recommend an appropriate life insurance product, considering the following factors:

- **Need for life insurance**

- **Types of life insurance**

- **Sources of life insurance**

- **Life insurance contractual provisions and riders**

Key Points:

To successfully complete this case study, students should use several steps of analysis to determine life insurance needs. They should also consider types and sources of life insurance, contractual provisions, and additional riders that could be used to tailor coverage for specific needs.

Key Words and Phrases:

Key Words

Needs approach
Method used to determine an adequate amount of life insurance based on the survivors' needs and the amount of existing life insurance, financial assets, and expected Social Security benefits.

Human life value approach
A mathematical computation used to determine how much life insurance is needed by valuing a human life.

Convertible
Characteristic of a term insurance policy that allows the policy to be exchanged for some type of permanent life insurance policy with no evidence of insurability.

Whole life insurance
Life insurance that provides lifetime protection, accrues cash value, and has premiums that remain unchanged during the insured's lifetime.

Universal life insurance
Flexible premium permanent life insurance that separates the protection, savings, and expense components.

Variable life insurance
A form of life insurance providing a death benefit that may change with time due to its variable cash value.

Variable universal life insurance
A form of universal life insurance that allows the policyholder to make fund choices for the investment component but that has no guaranteed cash value and no guaranteed interest rate.

Term life insurance
Life insurance that provides coverage for a specified period, such as ten or twenty years, with no cash value.

Universal life insurance
Insurance that provides life insurance protection and a savings component.

Beneficiary
Person(s) designated in a life insurance policy to receive the death benefit.

Grace period
Provision that continues a life insurance policy in force for a certain number of days (usually thirty or thirty-one) after the premium due date, during which time the policyowner can pay the overdue premium without penalty.

Incontestable clause
Clause that states that the insurer cannot contest the policy after it has been in force for a specified period, such as two years, during the insured's lifetime.

Nonforfeiture options
Provisions in a life insurance policy that give the policyowner a choice of ways to use the cash value if the policy is terminated and that protect the policyowner from forfeiting the cash value.

Reinstatement clause
A reinsurance treaty clause that reinstates the treaty's original per occurrence limit after a loss occurrence for a predetermined premium, subject to a maximum recovery for the contract year.

Settlement options
Various ways of paying life insurance policy proceeds to the beneficiary.

Suicide clause
Clause that states the insurer will not pay the death benefit if the insured commits suicide within a certain period (usually two years) after policy inception.

Rider
Similar to an endorsement; modifies a life insurance policy.

Accidental death benefit
Provision in a life insurance policy that doubles (or triples) the face amount of insurance payable if the insured dies as a result of an accident.

Guaranteed insurability rider (guaranteed purchase option)
Rider that permits the policyowner to buy additional amounts of life insurance at standard rates without evidence of insurability.

Retirement Planning

11

Educational Objective 1
Describe the financial impact of the retirement personal loss exposure on individuals and families.

Key Points:

Individuals and families face the loss exposure of outliving their financial resources in retirement. When individuals and families plan for retirement, they should determine the financial resources required for future expenses that will arise after income from full-time employment ends. Such planning should account for the effects of inflation and the future value of the dollar on retirement savings.

Study Tips

Pace your study. Don't cram.

A. Retirement Loss Exposures

Actual retirement funding losses are influenced by these factors:

1. Planning effectively

   a. This planning involves estimating the living expenses that will arise after income from full-time employment ceases and the anticipated length of retirement.

   b. Some individuals erroneously assume that expenses will decrease in retirement.

     • Healthcare costs usually increase as people age.

     • Planning should consider the potential costs of long-term care and the expenses related to spending more time on a hobby, recreational activity, or travel.

   c. Failure to accurately plan for retirement needs can result in a lower standard of living or the need to continue to working.

2. Accumulating sufficient retirement funds

   a. The objective of effective retirement planning is to accumulate sufficient funds to meet expenses and to maintain an acceptable standard of living.

   b. Individuals must supplement the minimal income Social Security provides with additional sources of retirement income, such as retirement and pension plans.

    c. In recent years, employers have moved away from defined benefit pension plans in favor of defined contribution plans.

- As a result of this trend, individuals must assume responsibility for establishing and/or contributing to their own retirement plans.
- Some employer plans are funded exclusively by employees, while others are funded by employees and employers.

    d. Individuals may use personal savings and investments, annuities, individual retirement accounts (IRAs), and cash value from life insurance policies to supplement their retirement savings.

3. Aging population

    a. The proportion of the United States population over age sixty-five is expected to increase from 12.4 percent in 2000 to 19.6 percent in 2030.

    b. This growth in the number of older individuals threatens to place a strain on the Social Security and healthcare systems.

    c. Members of this generation are expected to live longer than previous generations and, therefore, spend more years in retirement.

    d. Members of the baby boom generation (those born between 1946 and 1964) face several obstacles to adequately funding their retirement expenses.

- They must use methods other than Social Security to accumulate the savings required to meet retirement expense needs. This may mean working full-time beyond a planned retirement age or considering part-time employment.
- The financial situation of many baby boomers whose retirement plans included investments in equities changed dramatically as a result of global financial crisis starting in 2008.
- The decline in housing values also affected baby boomers.

4. The effect of inflation

    a. The inflation rate is a reflection of the increase in pricing levels for goods and services.

    b. Rising prices are especially problematic for retirees whose income is fixed.

    c. Goods and services such as healthcare, assisted living, long-term care, and prescription drugs are especially sensitive to higher inflation rates.

d. During inflationary periods, interest rates tend to rise, which can negatively affect the overall economy.

e. The effect of inflation on the future value of the dollar must be considered from the current planning period through the retirement age period.

Educational Objective 2
Describe strategies that financial planners use to assist individuals in investing for retirement.

Key Points:

Retirement planning entails adopting a structured approach to investing that will ensure sufficient income throughout retirement.

A. Basic Principles and Strategies

1. The first principle of retirement planning is to start saving as early as possible.

2. Another important principle financial planners follow is to adopt a long-term investment approach that entails regular investments throughout a working career.

   a. As an individual's earnings increase, contributions to retirement savings should increase accordingly.

   b. One good strategy is to immediately allot a portion of a salary increase or bonus to retirement savings.

3. Individuals should take advantage of defined contribution retirement accounts offered by employers as early as possible, when available, such as 401(k) and 403(b) plans.

   a. Such accounts are especially beneficial when an employer offers a matching contribution based on the employee's participation.

   b. Contributions to these retirement accounts reduce an individual's taxable income, because taxes on payroll deductions for these plans are deferred until the proceeds are withdrawn in retirement.

4. When an individual changes jobs, it is important to enroll in the new employer's retirement plan as soon as possible.

   a. Many employers require employees to have worked for a minimum period before they may participate in their retirement plan.

   b. During such a waiting period, an employee should "roll over" any retirement funds from previous employers to an individual retirement account (IRA) and continue to make regular contributions.

   c. In many cases, these combined savings can be rolled over to the new employer's retirement plan.

5. Although many employer-sponsored retirement plans include loan provisions, most financial planners advise against borrowing from retirement accounts, except in dire emergencies.

6. Most employer-sponsored retirement plans are participant-directed plans that allow employees to decide how their retirement funds will be invested.
   a. Generally, available options include a variety of mutual funds that invest in stocks, bonds, money market accounts, or a combination of them.
   b. Publicly held employers may also include the option of investing in company stock.
7. An employee's fund allocation should be based on his or her personal risk tolerance.
   a. Younger investors' investment strategies may be more aggressive because the effects of volatility in their portfolios will smooth out over time.
   b. Older investors should modify their approach to be more conservative as retirement age approaches.
   c. Regardless of risk tolerance, individuals should always diversify their investments to protect their earnings over time. Diversification allows poor returns from one type of investment to be offset by gains in another type of investment.

B. Lifecycle Funds
   1. These funds allow individuals to choose a targeted retirement date (such as 2020 or 2040) based on their current age and anticipated retirement age.
   2. Each fund consists of investments that appropriately match the strategy required for a specific age group.

C. Three-Legged Stool of Retirement Savings
   1. The three-legged stool is a traditional approach financial planners use in retirement planning for their clients.
   2. The three legs of the stool represent the major sources of retirement funds: Social Security benefits; pensions, employer-sponsored and other retirement plans; and personal savings.
   3. This concept has changed over time as concerns develop about future funding for Social Security benefits.
   4. The steady decline of defined benefit pension plans and the growth of defined contribution plans have also shifted the balance of the stool.
   5. The third leg, personal savings, may be the weakest, with personal savings participation in the United States at consistently low levels.
   6. The three-legged approach has value in reinforcing the idea that a balance of sources is required to adequately fund living expenses in retirement.

Educational Objective 3

Describe each of the following regarding retirement investing:

- **Basic types of investment objectives**

- **Types of investment risks**

- **Types of investments**

Key Points:

To achieve personal financial goals, an investor must decide which investment objectives and corresponding investment strategy are most important. The investor should learn about and consider the types of investment risks that funds will be exposed to when deciding which type of investment to purchase and retain.

A. Basic Types of Investment Objectives

Many investors, depending in part on their risk tolerance, will select one or more of the basic types of investment objectives to pursue:

1. Capital appreciation

    a. Many investors who consider capital appreciation to be their primary objective have a long-term investment horizon.

    b. An investor who is pursuing this objective will typically retain ownership of the investment, such as stock of a particular company, for an extended period and will reinvest dividends to purchase more shares. He or she may also make regular purchases in the same investment.

2. Preservation of capital

    a. This objective focuses less on increasing the value of investments and more on maintaining their value. This frequently results in a low rate of return.

    b. Investors with a short-term investment horizon may select this objective.

    c. To preserve the purchasing power of invested funds, investors pursuing this objective should select investments with a rate of return that at least matches the rate of inflation.

3. Current income

    a. Some investors prefer to place a higher priority on generating income from their investments than on long-term capital appreciation.

    b. They must be willing to expose their funds to higher risk in order to generate income.

    c. Purchasing real estate rental property that could provide steady current income fits this objective's investment strategy.

4. Growth and income

    a. Some investors seek both capital appreciation (growth) and current income (income).

    b. This combination can result in a high total rate of return but comes with a higher level of risk that the investment will lose value.

    c. Purchasing a company's stock that pays dividends and shows potential for capital appreciation fits this objective's investment strategy.

5. Liquidity

    a. The ability to quickly sell an investment with minimal loss of principle can allow an investor to meet sudden obligations that require cash.

    b. An example of a highly liquid investment is a savings account.

6. Minimization of taxes

    a. High-income investors will often place a priority on investments whose earnings are not taxed even though the rate of return may be lower than that of comparable investments.

    b. The purpose is to obtain a tax savings large enough to offset the lower rate of return, which would result in a higher net rate of return after taxes are taken into consideration.

    c. Investors who are concerned about minimizing taxes should maintain records of an investment's tax basis, which is the purchase price plus commissions and other expenses incurred to obtain ownership in an investment.

B. Types of Investment Risks

Investors should be aware of the different types of investment risk before they invest. Some of the more common risks that affect investors include these:

1. Purchasing power (or inflation) risk

This is the risk concerning the purchasing power of the proceeds from an investment. If the overall price levels in the economy increase, the purchasing power declines. If the price levels decrease, the purchasing power rises.

2. Market risk

This is the risk associated with fluctuations in prices of financial securities, such as stocks and bonds.

3. Interest-rate risk

This is the risk associated with price changes of existing investments due to changes in the general level of interest rates in the capital markets.

4. Maturity risk

This is the risk associated with securities that may mature at a time when interest rates in the capital markets are lower than those provided by the maturing investments, causing the investor to reinvest at a lower rate of interest.

5. Financial (or credit) risk

This is the risk that issuers of investments may have financial difficulties and, as a result, may not pay investors as expected. This risk includes the possibilities that the issuer of an investment could default, reduce or eliminate dividends, and file for bankruptcy.

6. Business risk

This is the risk associated with the nature of the industry in which the issuer of an investment operates and the management of the issuer itself.

7. Liquidity risk

This is the risk that an asset may not be easily or quickly convertible into cash at a reasonable price.

8. Investment manager risk

This is the risk associated with the variability in performance of persons responsible for managing an investor's assets.

C. Types of Investments

Some of the more commonly used investments for retirement planning include these:

1. Savings instruments

   a. Commercial banks and other financial institutions offer a variety of savings instruments that are free of market risk, interest-rate risk, and, when insured by the Federal Deposit Insurance Corporation (FDIC), financial (or credit) risk.

   b. The main advantage of savings instruments is their high liquidity.

   c. Purchasing power (or inflation) risk must be considered because the rate of return at times has been too low to keep pace with the cost of inflation.

   d. Four commonly used forms of this type of investment are savings accounts, certificates of deposit (CDs), money market mutual funds, and money market deposit accounts.

2. Stocks

   a. Investors who purchase stock in a corporation hold an ownership interest in the corporation and own a portion of its profits and losses.

     • If a corporation is profitable, the price of the investor's stock will normally rise and investors may receive regular divided payments.

     • When a corporation is unprofitable, the price of its stock usually falls and investors may receive lower or no dividend payments.

   b. Because stock prices can go up or down dramatically in a relatively short period, stocks are the most risky of the commonly used types of investment.

3. Bonds

   a. Governments and corporations sell bonds to raise funds to finance a project.

   b. Bonds are certificates of debt that include the seller's promise to pay investors a fixed amount on a fixed maturity date. The promise typically includes interest payments at fixed intervals at a fixed (coupon) rate of interest.

   c. The expected rate of return earned on a bond is higher than that of a savings account but lower than that of stock.

   d. Governments face a lower financial risk than corporations because they usually have taxing authority to generate the revenue needed to pay their obligations and they consequently have a lower rate of return.

4. Mutual funds

   a. Normally, a mutual fund is an actively-managed pool of funds from a group of investors.

     • A professional mutual fund manager invests the funds in a combination of stocks, bonds, or money market accounts based on the investment objectives of the investors.

     • Because a mutual fund owns a variety of investments, the risks associated with any one investment are diluted. This dilution is referred to as diversification.

   b. Some mutual funds, such as Index funds and lifecycle (or target date) funds, are passively managed. Index funds are considered to be passively managed because the fund manager does not try to out perform the market. Instead, the fund manager tries only to follow an index such as the Standard & Poor's 500 or Wilshire 5000.

5. Annuities

   a. Annuities are contracts sold by insurance companies.

    b. In return for a lump sum payment or a series of payments to the insurance company, the investor receives lifelong income through regular payments, usually after retirement.

6. Real estate

    a. Despite the variations and uncertainty of the housing market, an investor will benefit from shelter and security provided by a house.

    b. However, those benefits typically are not provided by other real estate investments which can create burdens beyond the initial investment, such as dealing with complex tax issues and difficult tenants.

Educational Objective 4
Compare the characteristics of traditional IRAs and Roth IRAs.

Key Points:

Traditional and Roth individual retirement accounts (IRAs) provide alternative investment options if an employer's retirement plan does not fit an individual's needs, or when an individual is seeking a tax break or wants to reduce his or her tax burden in retirement.

A. Traditional IRA

The Employee Income Retirement Security Act (ERISA) of 1974 created what is known as a traditional IRA. The IRA was originally established so individuals without employer-sponsored pension plans could save for retirement. This account has several distinct advantages that may make it an attractive investment even for an individual who has an employer-sponsored retirement plan available.

1. Eligibility

   a. To be eligible to invest in a traditional IRA, an individual must have earned taxable compensation during the year and be less than seventy and one-half years in age at the end of the year during which the investment is made.

   b. Taxable compensation includes wages, salaries, tips, commissions, fees, bonuses, self-employment income, taxable alimony, and separate maintenance payments.

   c. If an individual is covered by an employer retirement plan, the tax deductibility, but not the eligibility to invest, may be limited or eliminated.

2. Contributions

   a. For 2010, annual IRA contributions are limited to $5,000 or a maximum of 100 percent of taxable compensation, whichever is less.

   b. If the individual has a nonworking spouse, a spousal IRA (two separate IRAs at $5,000 each) is available with a maximum annual contribution of $10,000.

   c. If the contributing individual or spouses are fifty years or older, the contribution limit is raised to $6,000 per individual.

3. Tax treatment of contributions

   a. Contributions to a traditional IRA can be deducted when an IRA owner is calculating the amount owed in federal income taxes under two circumstances.

      • An individual who is not currently a participant in an employer-sponsored retirement plan can make an IRA contribution that is deductible up to the maximum annual limit.

      • An individual who is a participant in an employer's retirement plan can deduct up to the maximum annual limit for an IRA contribution if his or her modified adjusted gross income (an individual's adjusted gross income that does not take any IRA deduction into account) is below a certain limit.

   b. For the year 2010, a deduction up to the maximum annual limit is allowed if the taxpayer's modified adjusted gross income is $56,000 or less for individuals, or $89,000 or less for a married couple filing jointly.

   c. The deduction for a contribution of the maximum annual limit is incrementally phased out as modified adjusted gross income increases.

      • For the year 2010, the phase-out occurs between $56,000 to $66,000 for single taxpayers and $89,000 to $109,000 for married taxpayers filing jointly.

      • The phase-out limits are expected to slowly increase in the future.

   d. If an individual has an income above the phase-out limits, he or she can still contribute to a traditional IRA but will not be able to deduct his or her contributions when calculating the amount owed in federal income taxes.

4. Distributions

   a. Owners of IRAs are assessed a penalty if they take out distributions before they are fifty-nine and one-half years of age.

   b. To avoid other penalties, an owner must start receiving distributions at no later than seventy and one-half years of age.

5. Tax treatment of distributions

   a. The funds in a traditional IRA appreciate and earn interest on a tax-deferred, not tax-free, basis. As such, distributions are taxed as ordinary income if no penalty applies.

b. If a distribution is made before the owner of the IRA has reached age fifty-nine and one-half, a 10 percent tax penalty will be applied. However, this penalty may be waived if one of these exceptions applies:

- The distribution is made after the death or disability of the owner.
- The distribution is used to pay the health insurance deductible for medical care.
- The distribution is used to pay the health insurance premiums of an owner who becomes unemployed.
- The distribution is used to pay for qualified higher education expenses for the owner or a family member.
- The distribution is used to purchase the IRA owner's first home, subject to a $10,000 limit.
- The payment was part of a series of equal payments that are made at least every year for the life expectancy of the owner.

B. Roth IRA

The Taxpayer Relief Act of 1997 created the Roth IRA, which has fewer and different conditions than those of a traditional IRA.

1. Eligibility

    a. To be eligible to invest in a Roth IRA, an owner must have earned taxable compensation during the year.

    b. The age of the owner does not matter.

    c. It is possible to earn too much income to be eligible to invest in a Roth IRA. The maximum annual contribution can be made by single filers whose modified adjusted gross incomes are $105,000 or less, and by married couples filing jointly whose modified adjusted gross incomes are $166,000 or less.

- In 2010, maximum annual contributions are phased out for single taxpayers with modified annual gross incomes between $105,000 and $120,000.
- Maximum annual contributions are also phased out for married couples filing jointly with modified adjusted gross incomes between $167,000 and $177,000 for 2010.

2. Contributions

Annual contribution limits for a Roth IRA are the same as those for a traditional IRA; however, unlike a traditional IRA, contributions to a Roth IRA are made with funds that have already been taxed.

3. Tax treatment of contributions

Annual contributions to a Roth IRA are not income-tax deductible for any amount, regardless of participation in an employer sponsored retirement plan or level of income.

4. Distributions

   a. Penalty-free distributions of earnings cannot be made before the owner is fifty nine and one-half years of age.

   b. Roth IRAs impose no penalty if the owner does not start receiving distributions before reaching age seventy and one-half. There are no required distributions due to age. Therefore the funds of the owner can continue to accumulate tax-free.

5. Tax treatment of distributions

   a. Because the contributions, but not earnings, were made with after-tax dollars, they can be withdrawn from the Roth IRA without subjecting the owner to any additional federal income tax or penalty even if the owner has not reached fifty nine and one-half years of age.

   b. The earnings made on the contributions can also be withdrawn tax free and without a penalty, but only if the IRA has been in existence for five years or more and the owner is at least fifty nine and one-half years of age. If these conditions are not complied with, the earnings withdrawn will be taxed as ordinary income and a ten percent penalty will be applied.

   c. The tax and penalty may be waived if one of these exceptions applies:

      • The IRA owner becomes disabled (no penalty to owner).
      • The IRA owner dies (no penalty to beneficiaries).
      • The withdrawn funds are used to purchase the IRA owner's first home, subject to a $10,000 limit.

Educational Objective 5

Summarize the following types of tax-deferred retirement plans:

- **401(k) plan**

- **Profit-sharing plan**

- **Thrift plan**

- **Keogh plan**

- **403(b) plan**

- **SIMPLE (Savings Incentive Match Plan for Employees) plan**

- **ESOP (Employee Stock Ownership Plan)**

- **SEP (Simplified Employee Pension) plan**

Key Points:

Understanding the major characteristics of various qualified retirement plans offered by employers will help individuals decide which employment opportunity is best for them.

A. 401(k) Plan

1. Section 401(k) of the Internal Revenue Code allows employees to contribute a portion of their pre-tax salary to a qualified plan. Employers often make matching contributions.

2. Payment of income tax on contributions and the earnings from those contributions is deferred until withdrawals are made, which usually occurs during retirement.

3. To help to lower the costs and raise the consistency of investing, the contributions are made automatically through payroll deductions.

4. For the year 2010, annual contributions cannot exceed $16,900.

   a. If the employee is fifty years of age or older, he or she can make an additional catch-up contribution of $5,500.

   b. Both the $16,500 and $5,500 amounts will be increased in $500 increments in subsequent years as needed to counter inflation.

5. Withdrawal of funds without penalty is allowed only for one of these reasons:

   a. Attainment of age fifty nine and one-half years or older

   b. Separation from employment

    c. Death or disability

    d. Hardship for the employee as defined by the IRS

B. Thrift Plan

    1. A thrift (or savings) plan allows an employee to contribute a certain percentage of his or her salary, which the employer will then match to some extent, usually a percentage of what the employee contributed.

    2. If the employer limits the amount it will match or contribute, employees may be allowed to make an additional contribution that is unmatched by the employer.

    3. Thrift plans can be partially funded with before-tax or after-tax contributions, which are usually deducted from the employee's payroll.

    4. If the plan is funded with before-tax contributions, it is subject to the same restrictions as a 401(k) plan.

C. Profit-Sharing Plan

    1. The purpose of a profit-sharing plan is to distribute a percentage of an employer's profit among participating employees.

    2. Contributions by an employer can be made regardless of whether it has made a profit in the current or prior years.

    3. An employer's annual contributions are allocated to individual employees' accounts according to a pre-established formula, which may be based on each participant's compensation or on each participant's compensation and age.

    4. Whichever basis for the formula is used, total contributions cannot exceed 25 percent of the total covered compensation.

    5. Because contributions are made by the employer and are discretionary, an employee cannot be sure what amounts, if any, will be contributed to the plan in any one year.

    6. An employer can create its own restrictions on withdrawal of funds. These are common restrictions:

        a. Vesting for a certain number of years

        b. Reaching a certain age

        c. Retirement

        d. Termination of employment

        e. Death, disability, or illness

D. Keogh Plan

    1. Sole proprietors and business partners are prevented from participating in the qualified tax-deferred retirement plans available to their employees.

2. Keogh plans were developed to give owners of unincorporated businesses and other self-employed individuals the same tax advantages when investing for retirement as their employees. Their employees can also participate.

3. To be eligible, a self-employed individual must have earned income in the current year.

4. Contributed amounts are deducted from the individual's gross income on his or her individual tax return.

5. Self-employed individuals who establish Keogh plans may use the rules of another plan, such as a profit-sharing or 401(k) plan, to provide structure on how to administer the contributions and withdrawals.

E. 403(b) Plan

1. Section 403(b) of the Internal Revenue Code allows an employee of a tax-exempt organization that operates solely for charitable, religious, scientific, or educational purposes to invest in a tax-sheltered annuity.

2. The annuity is tax sheltered because the contributions are made with before-tax compensation.

3. Contributions are treated much the same as in a 401(k) plan.

F. SIMPLE Plan

1. SIMPLE plans are meant to encourage employers with 100 or fewer employees to establish qualified retirement plans.

2. These employers are exempt from administrative requirements that other plans impose.

3. Employees contribute before-tax compensation through payroll deductions, and the employer makes matching contributions for its eligible employees.

4. To be eligible, an individual must be paid at least $5,000 from the employer in the preceding year.

5. For the year 2010 the limit of total contributions was $11,500, although participants aged fifty years or older may make an additional catch-up contribution of $2,500.

6. When offering a SIMPLE plan, employers are not allowed to sponsor another qualified retirement plan.

7. Withdrawals are taxed as ordinary income and subject to a penalty if withdrawn before the employee reaches fifty nine and one half years of age.

G. ESOP

    1. ESOPs are qualified retirement plans that operate much like profit-sharing plans, with two primary differences.

        a. In an ESOP, the employer's contributions are not dependent on whether it has made a profit.

        b. ESOP contributions may be in the form of cash or employer's stock. If stock cannot be easily sold on an established market, the employee must be allowed to sell it back to the employer at its fair market value. The value of either form of contribution is limited to 25 percent of payroll.

    2. If the contribution is in the form of stock and it cannot be easily sold on an established market, the employee must be allowed to sell it back to the employer at its fair market value.

H. SEP Plan

    1. This is essentially a form of a traditional individual retirement account (IRA) that enables employers to make contributions to their employees' retirement accounts or, if self-employed, fund their own retirement accounts.

    2. SEPs differ from traditional IRAs in several ways.

        a. The annual contribution limit is much higher for a SEP than for an IRA. The limit for the year 2010 was $49,000 or 25 percent of each employee's compensation, whichever was less.

        b. An employer must contribute to the employee's SEP if the employee is at least twenty-one years of age and has worked for the employer in the current year and in three of the last five years.

    3. The income tax on an employer's contributions and the earnings on those contributions is deferred until withdrawal, at which time they are taxed as ordinary income. Withdrawals are subject to the same restrictions as with a traditional IRA.

Educational Objective 6

Describe the following types of employer-sponsored retirement plans:

- **Defined Benefit**
- **Defined Contribution**
- **Defined Benefit 401(k) Plans**

Key Points:

Each of these types of plans has distinguishing characteristics in terms of what is contributed, the benefits paid, and the risks and advantages to the employee and employer.

A. Defined Benefit Plans

1. These are sponsored by an employer, who is responsible for providing a fixed monthly benefit at the time of an employee's retirement.
   a. The amount the employer must contribute varies depending on the investment earnings on the contributions.
   b. Typically the employee makes no contributions to the plan.
2. The amount of the benefit is usually based on a formula that takes into account the number of years an employee has worked for the employer.
   a. The amount of salary used in the formula varies from employer to employer.
   b. Payment of benefits starts when the employee retires and continues for as long as he or she lives.
   c. Ancillary benefits may also be provided for early retirement, termination, death, disability, or another event that ends employment before the normal retirement age of sixty-five years.
3. There are risks that an employee will not receive the full benefit amount promised by the employer:
   a. The employee might not remain employed by the employer until retirement age.
   b. The plan could be terminated by the employer.
   c. The employer might not contribute sufficient funds.
4. Many risks can be partially mitigated through ancillary benefits, placing contributions in a pension trust, or having terminated plan benefits guaranteed by the Pension Benefit Guaranty Corporation.

B. Defined Contribution Plans

    1. In these, the sponsoring employer is responsible for contributing a fixed matching percentage of the contributions an employee makes.

    2. A common example of a defined contribution plan is a 401(k) plan, in which an employer might match up to 50 percent of an employee's 4 percent salary contribution.

    3. The employer does not promise that a fixed monthly benefit will be available upon the employee's retirement.

        a. The employer's contribution remains the same, and it is the benefits received by the employee that vary.

        b. If an employee wants a benefit that is high enough to replace a certain percentage of his or her earnings decrease on retirement, the employee, not the employer, will have to increase contributions to make up the difference.

    4. Defined contribution plans force employees to assume the investment risk of earnings volatility.

    5. No additional funds are payable by the employer if an employee dies, becomes disabled, or is terminated before retirement age.

    6. It is often easier for employers to administer and explain the benefits of a defined contribution plan than of a defined benefit plan.

    7. Defined contributions plans are becoming more common than defined benefit plans. The global financial crisis that began in 2008 has accelerated the trend.

C. Defined Benefit 401(k) Plans

    1. To reverse the trend toward defined contribution plans, Congress passed the 2006 Pension Protection Act to create the defined benefit 401(k) plan.

    2. A defined benefit 401(k) plan, also called the DB (k), is a combination of a defined benefit plan and a defined contribution plan that offers the benefits of a 401(k) savings plan along with a guaranteed flow of income.

    3. To be eligible, the employer must have between two employees and five hundred employees.

    4. The plan must have a defined benefit portion of 1 percent of an employee's average salary per year of service, up to twenty years.

    5. It must also have a defined contribution portion that automatically enrolls employees in a 401(k) plan with a 4 percent contribution unless they decline to participate.

    6. The employer must match at least half of the employee's 401(k) contribution, up to 2 percent of the employee's salary.

7. Vesting for the defined benefit portion occurs after three years of service. As a result, the funds stay with the employer if an employee is terminated before three years.

8. For the defined contribution 401(k) portion, vesting occurs immediately.

9. Withdrawals at retirement are made as monthly checks similar to a traditional pension plan.

10. Some of the advantages for employers are less paperwork, fewer regulations, and less cost compared to operating a defined benefit plan and a 401(k) separately.

Educational Objective 7
Summarize the various types of individual annuities.

Key Points:

An annuity is a type of life insurance policy or contract that makes periodic payments to the recipient for a fixed period or for life in exchange for a specified premium. Group annuities (or qualified annuities) are provided by organizations to employees for retirement funding benefits. Individual annuities (or nonqualified annuities) are sold to the general public and are often used as tax-deferred investment vehicles.

The period during which the benefits are paid is called the payout period. The payout amount, or cash value, is made up of the premium (principal) and the interest earned over the life of the annuity. Each periodic payment (benefit) includes a portion of both principal and interest, and it might include a survivor benefits amount as provided by the annuity contract. When the annuitant dies, the premium is entirely liquidated and nothing or very little remains for the heirs. This is called the mortality risk of life annuities.

Various types of annuities can be purchased in the market. There are three fundamental classifications.

A. Annuity Types Based on the Starting Date of the Annuity

   1. Deferred annuities

      a. The period between the owner's purchase of the annuity and the annuitant's age at which benefit payments begin is called the accumulation period.

      b. Benefits are not payable until a specified year in the future, such as when the annuitant reaches a certain age or after a specified number of years.

      c. The cash value component of an annuity benefit is not taxable to the annuitant, and only the interest component is subject to federal income tax as ordinary income.

      d. Deferred annuities are preferred for retirement planning, as they enable the annuity owner to make premium payments during the accumulation period—which accumulate tax-deferred interest—for periodic payout over the annuitant's lifetime.

e. If the annuitant on a deferred annuity dies before any payout is made on the contract, the annuitant's beneficiaries end up paying ordinary income taxes on the earnings as opposed to paying inheritance taxes on the distribution.

2. Immediate annuities

   a. Benefit payments begin soon after the annuity owner purchases the annuity.

   b. Immediate annuities typically do not earn as much investment interest as the earnings from deferred annuities.

   c. Immediate annuities provide fewer tax-deferred interest earnings, and the annuitant pays less ordinary income tax on the early payouts when they are received.

3. For individual/nonqualified annuity policies issued after January 18, 1985, any taxable amount received or withdrawn before age fifty-nine and one-half is generally subject to a 10 percent federal early withdrawal penalty, with a few exceptions, such as the death or disability of the annuity's owner as well as immediate annuities.

4. If an individual purchases an annuity as part of his or her retirement planning, he or she would be the annuity owner, annuitant, and beneficiary.

   a. Annuities can have multiple annuitants, such as an individual and his or her spouse.

   b. They can have multiple beneficiaries; for example, a spouse or children may be listed as beneficiaries.

   c. An annuity might be purchased to provide income for another individual. The purchaser would be the annuity owner, and the recipient would be the annuitant and beneficiary.

5. The cost of and benefits provided by annuities based on a single life are determined by the characteristics of the annuitant, such as age, health, and life expectancy. Similar characteristics are considered for any additional beneficiaries.

6. A joint-and-last-survivor annuity is designed to provide payouts to all annuitants throughout their lifetimes. The less-popular joint life annuity provides payouts to two or more annuitants until one annuitant dies; then no further payouts are made.

7. The premium cost for an annuity for a specified amount of income benefits depends on the combined length of the accumulation and payout periods.

   a. An annuity with shorter accumulation and payout periods (such as one purchased by an older individual) earns less interest than one with longer accumulation and payout periods (such as one purchased by a younger individual).

    b. The cost is lower with shorter accumulation and payout periods because the insurer does not have to pay as much in total benefits.

    c. Because the insurer's payout periods could be longer when multiple beneficiaries are involved, costs for these annuities are higher than those for annuities for a single beneficiary.

B. Annuity Types Based on the Party That Bears the Investment Risk
The party that bears the investment risk can choose from a variety of investments to best match the investor's objectives. Generally, the party that bears the investment risk can be either the annuity owner or the insurer that provides the annuity. This classification includes four general types of annuities:

1. Fixed-dollar annuities

    a. The investment risk is borne by the insurer.

    b. An insurer typically invests its customers' fixed-dollar annuity premiums in securities such as bonds, real estate, and mortgages (investments that become part of the insurer's general assets) in exchange for a fixed rate of return.

    c. The value of the annuity does not fluctuate with market performance, but the interest rate can vary throughout the accumulation and payout periods.

    d. These are considered a more conservative investment than other types of annuities; therefore, they have a lower rate of return.

2. Variable annuities (VAs)

    a. The owner bears the investment risk.

    b. The VA owner chooses from a variety of investment funds, called subaccounts, into which they invest their annuity premiums to optimize their returns according to their investment time horizons.

    c. The insurer hires experts to manage these subaccounts, which are separate from the insurer's general assets. These subaccounts are protected from the insurer's creditors if the insurer becomes insolvent.

    d. When the payout period begins on the VA, the current value of the investment fund is converted into units. The annuity guarantees that a specified number of units will be paid periodically, but the value of each unit will vary as determined by the performance of the subaccounts.

3. Combination plans

    a. Combination plans combine features of fixed-dollar and variable annuities.

    b. The insurer might make the investment decisions in the interests of the annuity owner, but the annuity owner bears the investment risk.

  4. Equity indexed annuities (EIAs)

    a. The insurer bears the investment risk.

    b. EIAs are fixed-dollar annuities that limit the fluctuations in the cash value. They are linked to a stock market index, usually an equity index such as Standard & Poor's 500.

    c. The insurer guarantees payment of a minimum principal amount and a minimum interest earnings rate.

      • The value of the EIA investment return can increase with the market, based on the index values, but if the market fares poorly, the premium and interest rate will never drop below the guaranteed rates.

      • EIAs can exceed their guaranteed value at maturity.

    d. The variations and many intricacies of EIAs can make them less attractive to investors.

C. Annuity Types Based on Premium Payment Method

Two types of annuities are classified based on the premium payment method:

  1. Flexible-premium annuities

Flexible-premium annuities enable the annuity owner to decide when to pay periodic premiums.

    a. A flexible-premium deferred annuity (FPDA), has no pre-determined premium amount and no required payment frequency.

    b. Most require a minimum payment amount.

  2. Single-premium annuities

The owner of a single-premium annuity purchases the annuity using one lump-sum payment.

    a. A single-premium deferred annuity (SPDA) premium is paid well in advance of the payout period.

    b. A single-premium immediate annuity premium is paid shortly before the payout begins.

Educational Objective 8

Describe the following with regard to the United States Social Security program:

- **The basic characteristics of OASDHI**

- **Covered occupations**

- **The eligibility requirements for insured status**

- **The types of benefits provided**

Key Points:

The United States federal Social Security program, also known as OASDHI (old age, survivors, disability, and health insurance system), was designed to provide benefits to qualified individuals upon their retirement or if they become disabled and are unable to work, and to supplement medical care. Family members of an eligible worker may also receive certain benefits. The benefits provided by Social Security are minimal, however, and other sources of retirement income, disability income, and insurance are suggested to supplement Social Security payments.

A. Basic Characteristics of OASDHI

    1. Most working individuals are covered under the Social Security program for some benefits, and most are currently paying or will pay Social Security taxes based on their earnings.

    2. Workers are entitled to Social Security retirement benefits if they were fully insured at the age at which they retired.

        a. Social Security defines "fully insured" as having earned forty quarters of coverage. A quarter of coverage is earned for each quarter of a year that an individual works.

        b. Effectively, an individual is fully insured after ten full years of work; the quarters do not have to be consecutive as long as forty quarters are earned.

    3. Calculation of Social Security benefits is complicated; however, the Social Security Administration mails a benefit estimate statement to insured individuals every year.

    4. The Social Security Administration offers a Web site with tools to help individuals estimate their future financial needs, to identify the Social Security programs for which they might be eligible, to learn how their age at retirement and other types of earnings and pensions affect their Social Security benefits, and to answer many other questions.

B. Covered Occupations

   1. Individuals in most occupations, including self-employed individuals who earn $400 or more in one year, pay Social Security taxes and earn Social Security benefits.

   2. Certain occupations, such as self-employed workers, domestic service workers, ministers, and U.S. Government civilian workers, have special rules for calculating Social Security taxes and benefits.

   3. Some types of work or workers are not covered, including federal workers; foreign agricultural workers; and students performing service for a school, college, or university.

C. Eligibility Requirements for Insured Status

   1. To receive any Social Security benefits, an individual must have insured status.

      a. "Fully insured status" is one requirement for particular types of benefits; however, some benefits may apply if the individual qualifies as "currently insured."

      b. To qualify for disability benefits, an individual must have "disability-insured status."

   2. The government uses an individual's lifetime earnings record, reported under his or her Social Security number (SSN), to assign Social Security credits for a specified amount of work (a quarter) and to determine insured status.

   3. To be fully insured, an individual must have at least six credits and meet certain age requirements based on various dates at the time of retirement; however, no more than forty credits are required, regardless of the individual's birth date.

      a. An individual may earn no more than four credits in a year.

      b. The full retirement age is currently sixty-five. However, in 2003, the full retirement age began increasing from sixty-five to sixty-seven starting with individuals born in 1938.

   4. To qualify for currently insured status, an individual must have at least six Social Security credits during the full thirteen-quarter period that ends the year he or she dies, most recently becomes entitled to disability benefits, or becomes entitled to retirement insurance benefits.

   5. To qualify for disability status, an individual must have at least twenty credits during a forty-calendar-quarter period (called the 20/40 rule).

      a. The forty-calendar-quarter period ends in the quarter the individual is determined to be disabled, and he or she is fully insured in that calendar quarter.

   b. Individuals who are disabled before age thirty-one can qualify for disability insurance benefits as an option to the 20/40 rule, called "special insured status."

   c. Blind workers who are fully insured are not required to meet the 20/40 rule or the requirements for special insured status.

D. Types of Benefits Provided by Social Security

Social Security provides several possible benefits to insured individuals and/or their dependents. Except for Medicare, Social Security benefits are based on the individual's primary insurance amount (PIA). The PIA is calculated by applying a formula to the worker's average monthly earnings over a specified number of years. A family maximum benefit (FMB) is also calculated from the PIA to limit the benefit amount that may be paid to a worker and his or her eligible dependents.

1. Retirement (old age) benefits

   a. An individual can receive retirement (old age) benefits when he or she reaches age sixty-two and has attained fully insured status.

   b. The retirement insurance benefit equals the individual's PIA. In certain cases, a special minimum benefit is provided to some individuals who have had low earnings.

   c. A fully insured worker may begin receiving retirement benefits at age sixty-two (before the full-benefit retirement age), but the benefit amount would be permanently reduced. Optionally, a worker can elect to delay retirement until age seventy and receive increased benefits starting at age seventy.

   d. The spouse of a retired worker who has reached age sixty-two can receive a lifetime reduced retirement benefit that is 50 percent of the fully insured worker's PIA, up to the FMB.

   - If the worker retires at age sixty-five, the full spousal retirement benefit can be paid to the spouse.

   - If the spouse is entitled to a personal retirement benefit, then the spouse would receive the larger of his or her personal benefit or his or her spousal benefit.

   - Additional benefits may also be provided for each qualified dependent on the worker's retirement until the FMB has been met.

2. Survivors (death) benefits

These may be paid to the surviving spouse and other qualified dependents of a deceased worker who was fully insured at the time of his or her death.

    a. The surviving spouse qualifies for survivors benefits if he or she is at least age sixty or is disabled and at least age fifty.

- The surviving spouse can receive 100 percent of the deceased worker's survivor PIA if that spouse is full-benefit retirement age.
- The benefit amount is reduced for younger surviving spouses.

    b. Unmarried children and qualifying grandchildren of a deceased worker can receive a child's monthly survivors benefit.

- This benefit is generally 75 percent of the deceased parent's PIA.
- The child must be under age eighteen, or eighteen and an elementary or a secondary student, or eighteen or older but disabled before age twenty-two.

    c. A parent who was dependent on the insured worker before his or her death and who has reached age sixty-two can also receive a survivors benefit.

- If only one parent is entitled to benefits, the surviving parent's benefit is generally 82.5 percent of the deceased worker's PIA.
- If two parents are entitled to surviving parent's benefits, the benefit amount is generally 75 percent of the deceased worker's PIA.

    d. The surviving spouse who cares for an eligible child or grandchild receives a mother's or father's surviving spouse benefit. This benefit is generally 75 percent of the deceased worker's PIA.

    e. Note that all of these benefits combined are subject to the FMB.

    f. A lump-sum death benefit of $255 may be paid to the survivors of a worker who dies having met the fully insured or currently insured status. It is paid in addition to any monthly survivors benefits. Certain restrictions can apply.

3. Disability

    a. The Social Security disability income (SSDI) Monthly Cash Benefits are designed to replace a portion of a wage earner's income for a short period of time if the wage earner becomes disabled because of an injury or illness.

    b. A five-month waiting period applies before any benefits will be paid.

    c. Auxiliary benefits may be paid to the spouse and other dependents of the injured worker.

   d. An established "period of disability" under the Social Secu-
      rity law is a continuous period during which an individual is
      disabled.

   e. The established period of disability is not counted when
      determining an individual's insured status under Social
      Security and is not counted in determining the monthly
      benefit amount payable to the worker and his or her depen-
      dents.

4. Health insurance (Medicare)

   a. Under Social Security, people age sixty-five or older, those
      under sixty-five with certain disabilities, and people of all
      ages with specified medical conditions can qualify to receive
      federal Medicare health benefits including hospital insur-
      ance, medical insurance, and prescription drug coverage.

   b. Medicare beneficiaries can also choose to take advantage of
      Medicare Advantage plans that offer higher benefit levels
      and include managed-care plans and private fee-for-service
      plans.

Key Words and Phrases:

Key Words

Personal risk tolerance
An individual investor's degree of comfort with various levels of risk in investments.

Risk tolerance
The level of residual risk that an organization and its stakeholders are willing to bear within a given strategic context.

Capital appreciation (capital gain)
The amount by which an asset's selling price exceeds its purchase price.

Preservation of capital
Practice of ensuring that the value of assets does not decrease.

Liquidity
The ease with which an asset can be converted to cash with little or no loss of value.

Investment risk
Uncertainty of investment outcomes.

Traditional Individual Retirement Account (IRA)
A retirement savings plan by which an individual can use tax-deductible and tax-deferred methods for accumulating funds.

Roth IRA
A retirement savings plan by which an individual can accumulate investment income on a tax-free basis (subject to certain limitations).

Defined benefit plan
A pension plan that is based on the monthly retirement benefit rather than on the contribution rate.

Defined contribution plan
A pension plan in which the contribution is a percentage of the participating employee's earnings or a flat dollar amount.

Annuity
A type of life insurance policy or contract that makes periodic payments to the recipient for a fixed period or for life in exchange for a specified premium.

Disability and Health Insurance Planning

12

Educational Objective 1

Describe the financial impact of disability and other health-related personal loss exposures on individuals and families.

Key Points:

Study Tips

Rewriting key concepts in your own words can improve retention.

Sometimes people are injured outside of the workplace or become seriously ill, rendering them unable to report to their jobs for many months. For those without disability and health insurance, such injuries and illnesses can deplete a family's savings and lead to bankruptcy filing or mortgage foreclosure.

A. Disability Loss Exposures

   1. The chance that an individual will become disabled is greater than the chance of an early death.

   2. Most families do not have savings that would sustain them for a long-term disability and cover the associated medical and other costs.

   3. In addition to the loss of the disabled individual's wages, there are generally medical expenses to be paid (with or without health insurance), and the individual may incur costs for rehabilitation or for education so that he or she could qualify for another type of job in which the disability would not be a concern.

   4. The United States Social Security Administration survey results led to a 2007 estimate that more than 75 percent of Americans living in the U.S. are insured under the government's disability insurance program (available to much of the working population). However, there are limitations to the benefits in that program.

B. Health-Related Loss Exposures

   1. Many Americans do not have health insurance.

      a. Young, healthy individuals often do not recognize the need for such coverage or the financial benefit it can provide.

      b. Many lower-income, single-wage-earner families and elderly individuals do not purchase it due to the high cost and, often, lack of availability.

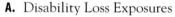

2. Private healthcare insurance is available to individuals who do not have group health insurance.

   a. Some are unaware that private plans exist.

   b. The cost of private health insurance for the benefits provided is significantly greater than the cost of group health insurance (as provided by an employer) because private plans lack the cost savings from economies of scale.

3. Associations offer group healthcare insurance plans with lower premiums.

   a. Generally, under private insurance and smaller group plans, individuals or associations select fewer benefits or higher copayments to save money on premiums.

   b. These plans might offer benefits only for lesser-quality medications and older treatment methods, often using outdated technology.

4. The costs of medical treatment often cause uninsured individuals to avoid medical treatment for illnesses or injuries until their health has deteriorated enough that more costly medical treatment is required.

5. Some illnesses require long-term care, and lower-income individuals are less likely to purchase long-term care insurance.

6. A disabled individual might lose his or her job, along with any healthcare insurance and disability benefits provided by the employer.

7. Individuals who have health insurance tend to live longer and have a better quality of life than uninsured individuals.

C. Long-Term Care Loss Exposures

   1. Individuals and families who have health insurance can still suffer financial difficulty or devastation because of the costs of long-term care for certain serious medical conditions.

   2. Individuals requiring long-term healthcare might need skilled nursing care after hospitalization or might need long-term in-home healthcare to assist them with their daily activities.

D. Insurance Treatment of Disability, Health-Related, and Long-Term Care Loss Exposures

   1. Unexpected, high medical costs; disability costs; and long-term care costs can easily exhaust an individual's or a family's savings and retirement funds.

      a. These costs can drive some individuals or families into bankruptcy and/or cause them to lose their homes and other possessions.

      b. Insurance options exist to help individuals and families better manage these financial loss exposures.

2. Various sources offer disability insurance, which replaces lost income when a wage earner becomes disabled. In some cases, multiple forms of disability insurance, such as private and government insurance, combine to provide the best coverage.

3. Health insurance is available from various sources to pay for routine and/or major medical expenses, such as limited hospitalization, surgery, and so forth. Individual and group plans and/or the government's plan (Medicare) may combine to provide the best coverage for individuals who qualify.

4. Long-term care insurance has emerged to pay the costs associated with treatment of a serious, long-term medical condition.

Educational Objective 2

Summarize the distinguishing characteristics of each of the following types of disability income insurance:

- **Individual disability income insurance**

- **Group disability income insurance**

- **Social Security Disability Income program**

Key Points:

An overview of these three types of disability income insurance provides insight into the products and options available to help wage earners avoid the financial duress that is often associated with disability:

- Individual disability income insurance
- Group disability income insurance
- Social Security Disability Income (SSDI) program

A. Provisions of a Disability Income Policy

  1. Benefit periods

    a. A disability income policy specifies a benefit period and a maximum benefit period.

- The benefit period is the time period for which benefits will be paid to a disabled individual (the insured). It ends when the insured "returns to work" or reaches the maximum benefit period.

- The maximum benefit period is the longest period for which benefits will be paid to the insured.

    b. Policies with maximum benefit periods that extend many years require higher premiums; therefore, when selecting a maximum benefit period, individuals must consider their financial needs, their own age, and the ages of their dependents, as well as weigh the benefits against costs.

  2. Perils insured against

    a. A disability income policy provides specified benefits in the event that the insured individual suffers any illness, accident, or injury that causes the individual to lose income.

    b. Some disability policies pay disability income benefits for certain types of permanent injuries, such as the loss of a limb or blindness.

3. Waiting period

    a. The waiting period is the time that elapses after a wage earner becomes disabled, before income benefits will be paid.

    b. The waiting period may be seven days for a short-term disability policy, or it may be thirty days, sixty days, ninety days, or one year or more for a long-term disability policy.

    c. Shorter waiting periods require higher insurance premiums to cover the insurer's costs.

    d. Employers who provide group disability income insurance often select a waiting period that takes effect when employees' short-term disability ends or sick leave has been exhausted.

4. Definition of disability

    a. This definition describes the extent of disability that is required for income payments to begin and might be based on the insured's inability to perform occupational duties, on the amount of earned income lost, or both.

    b. When the definition is based on the insured's inability to perform job duties, the description might refer to these terms:

        • The term "any occupation" means that the individual is totally disabled and unable to perform the duties of any occupation. A policy using this definition of disability will not pay benefits if the insured can perform the duties of another occupation or can attain the necessary education or training to perform the duties of a new occupation.

        • The term "own occupation" means the insured is unable to return to the duties of his or her specific occupation. If the insured is able to earn income from another occupation, he or she will still receive 100 percent of the disability benefits. Some policies use a modified definition so that if the insured is able to earn income from another occupation, the benefit payments are reduced.

        • Under a disability policy that uses a "split definition" for disability, the "any" and "own" occupation concepts are combined. For example, the policy might use an "any occupation" definition for the first six months of disability, and then it might revert to an "own occupation" definition if the disability extends beyond six months.

    c. When the definition of disability is based on the amount of earned income lost, a specified percentage of earned income lost will result in the payment of benefits.

      d. Some policies combine the two approaches in defining disability.

    5. Benefits provided

      The benefits provided tie together all of the policy features—such as the waiting period, the benefits periods, the perils insured against, and the definition of disability—with features such as the amount of coverage and the payment period (weekly, monthly), and any terms for coordination of benefits with other disability income policies.

    6. Renewal or continuance provision

      a. A noncancelable disability income policy can never be canceled by the insurer. The insurer cannot change the benefits provided, the rates, or other policy features unless the insured requests a change.

      b. A guaranteed renewable policy will continue as long as the premiums continue to be paid, up to a specified age, such as sixty-five or seventy, as long as the insured is gainfully employed (earning a reasonable salary).

        • The insurer must renew the policy at the insured's request.

        • The insurer reserves the right to raise premiums on renewal for reasons specified in the contract.

      c. A conditionally renewable policy provides that the insurer has an option to increase the premium and change the policy terms at renewal. This policy allows the insurer to cancel the contract if the conditions for renewal are not met.

B. Individual Disability Income Insurance

    1. Individual disability income insurance generally provides monthly benefits to a disabled wage earner for a selected period to reimburse the wage earner's income during a period of total or partial disability.

    2. Individual policies will usually replace 60 percent of an insured's lost income, and sometimes up to 70 or 80 percent under some plans.

    3. Individuals purchase individual disability income insurance, which is available to the public through insurance brokers and agents.

    4. Coverages and provisions under individual disability income insurance are typically the same as those for group insurance.

    5. Individuals can use a policy as primary coverage or supplemental to other disability income insurance.

6. Individual disability income insurance is purchased using after-tax dollars. Consequently, disability benefits that are paid from an individual policy are not taxable to the insured.

7. Some advantages of individual disability income insurance over group insurance are these:

   a. No membership in a group is required to purchase the coverage.

      • A job change will not affect coverage, so the insured can purchase a noncancelable policy at a young age, when premiums are lower, and continue the coverage until retirement or beyond.

      • Some individuals do not qualify for group disability income insurance because of tenure requirements before the benefit is available.

   b. Group and Social Security benefits may not be adequate to cover the insured's disability income needs. An individual disability income policy may be used to supplement other coverage provided.

8. Riders (options) are available for purchase with an individual disability income insurance policy. Premiums vary based on the payout.

C. Group Disability Income Insurance

   1. Group disability income insurance is made available through an employer or some type of association.

   2. Economies of scale enable the insurer to offer lower premiums to the insured individuals.

   3. Group disability income insurance generally provides weekly or monthly benefits for a selected period to reimburse the disabled wage earner's income during a period of total or partial disability.

   4. An employer may offer both short-term and long-term disability income insurance plans.

      a. Short-term plans might offer weekly benefits, with a short waiting period (one to seven days), and short maximum benefit periods.

      b. A long-term disability plan (often called LTD) might have a higher maximum benefit payout, such as $3,000 or $5,000 per month or $60,000 per year.

         • LTD policies usually replace around 60 percent of an insured's lost income.

         • The waiting period under an LTD plan might require a three-month to six-month wait for benefits to begin.

         • Most group LTD plans use a split definition of disability.

- Options are generally limited.
- Most LTD plans have a coordination-of-benefits provision that defines how disability income benefits from other plans, such as SSDI and state disability plans, will affect benefits paid by the LTD plan. These provisions generally do not account for individual disability income insurance.

5. Premiums are paid by the employer in part or in full, and premiums may be deducted from payroll on a before-tax basis; so benefits are taxed as ordinary income. Premiums are paid after taxes by the individual under an association's plan, so benefits are not taxable.

6. Generally, the group disability income coverage terminates when the individual's employment or association ends, if the employer fails to pay the premium for the employee, or if the group policy is terminated by the employer or association.

D. Social Security Disability Income Program

Rules to qualify under the Social Security Disability Income (SSDI) program are strict compared with other disability plans. The program provides monthly cash benefits and establishment of a period of disability for disabled workers.

1. Disability definition
   a. To be considered "disabled" under Social Security, a worker must be unable to engage in any substantial gainful activity because of a "medically determinable" physical or mental impairment as defined in the Social Security law.
      - A substantial gainful activity is one that requires significant activities that are physical, mental, or a combination of the two, in work that is performed for profit, even if no profit is realized.
      - This work will qualify whether it is full-time or part-time work.
   b. The worker's impairment must be established by objective medical evidence, and it must be expected to last for at least twelve consecutive months or to result in the individual's death.
   c. Special rules apply for blindness, and special circumstances related to the disability can disqualify an individual.

2. Monthly cash benefits
   a. Payment of benefits requires a five-month waiting period.
   b. The monthly cash benefit is generally equal to the primary insurance amount (PIA).
   c. Auxiliary benefits may also be provided for a qualified disabled worker's eligible dependents.

    d. Disabled worker benefits may be reduced, including the auxiliary benefits, to fully or partially offset any workers compensation benefit and any disability benefits received under a federal, state, or local disability plan.

    e. These benefits are subject to the Social Security Family Maximum Benefit (FMB).

3. Establishment of a disability period

    a. Establishment of a disability period is essential for determination of numerous Social Security benefits.

    b. A "period of disability" under the Social Security law is a continuous period during which an individual is disabled.

    c. A period of disability must be established during a worker's disability or within twelve months after the disability ends, assuming the worker has met "disability insured status" and the disability lasted at least five consecutive months. Special exceptions exist.

Educational Objective 3

Summarize the distinguishing characteristics of healthcare benefits provided by each of the following sources: individual, group, and government-provided health insurance plans.

Key Points:

Americans obtain the benefits of health insurance plans from three primary sources: individual, group, and government-provided health insurance plans.

A. Individual Health Insurance Plans

1. Less than nine percent of Americans purchase individual (non-group) health insurance.

2. Individual health insurance is the only coverage option for consumers who are not eligible for employer-sponsored group insurance or government-provided insurance.

3. The most prevalent providers of individual health insurance are commercial insurers and Blue Cross and Blue Shield plans.

4. These are the typical consumers of individual health plans:

   a. Young adults who are no longer on their parents' plans but are not covered under employer or college plans

   b. Workers who have left employment-based plans before reemployment

   c. People who are otherwise not in group plans but do not qualify for government programs

5. One type of policy favored by consumers in the individual health insurance market is a preferred provider organization (PPO) plan, which provides the standard basic medical and surgical care offered by other health plans.

6. Some insurers offer "niche" insurance plans or low-cost plans with restricted benefits.

7. For many consumers, periods of dependence on individual insurance are relatively short. Periods of dependence on individual health insurance are likely to be longer for older persons and those who are self-employed.

8. Insurers accept about 90 percent of applicants for nongroup insurance, and, of those, over 70 percent receive requested coverage at standard rates.

9. Nearly three-quarters of consumers who look into buying coverage in the individual market never purchase a plan, either because they cannot find one that fits their needs or that they can afford, or because insurers reject them because of preexisting conditions.

10. Health insurers use community rating of health benefits to set premiums that spread risk evenly across an entire policyholder community so that everyone pays the same rate regardless of age, health status, or claim history.

   a. Modified community rating limits the experience to a geographic area.

   b. Adjusted community rating is adjusted by factors specific to a particular group (such as an occupation or a kind of business). It leads to lower-risk consumers' paying a higher price for insurance than people with greater risks and gives consumers an incentive to wait to purchase health insurance until they need medical services.

11. The individual market's retail nature can involve multiple providers and partners in numerous one-on-one transactions, sometimes resulting in administrative inefficiency and causing risks to shift quickly and dramatically.

B. Group Health Insurance Plans

   1. The most prevalent group health insurance providers are commercial insurers, Blue Cross and Blue Shield plans, and self-insured plans.

   2. Most larger group health insurance plans are subject to experience rating so that each group pays according to its actual claim experience.

   3. Some smaller groups are community rated within their small-group communities.

   4. In a self-insurance plan, an employer assumes the financial risk for providing healthcare benefits to employees, paying for each claim as it is incurred instead of paying a premium to an insurer.

   a. The employer can either directly process the claims or contract with a third-party administrator (TPA) for claim processing.

   b. The employer can also customize the plan and contract directly with healthcare providers to meet the specific healthcare needs of its employees.

   c. Self-insured plans also are not subject to state health insurance premium taxes.

5. Certain important provisions, some required by law, apply to most group health insurance policies.

   a. A preexisting conditions clause, found in most group health insurance plans, excludes coverage for preexisting medical conditions for a limited period after an insured enters the plan.

   - A preexisting condition is a medical condition that existed before the plan's effective date.

   - After the waiting period expires, the condition is no longer considered preexisting and is covered subject to any other plan limitations.

   - In 1996, Congress enacted the Health Insurance Portability and Accountability Act (HIPAA), which prohibits employers and insurers that offer health insurance from dropping people from coverage because they are sick or from imposing waiting periods for preexisting conditions for more than a specified time period. HIPAA also guarantees employees who maintain continuous coverage, as defined by the act, can never be excluded because of a preexisting condition.

   b. To prevent overinsurance and benefit duplication, group health insurance typically contains a coordination-of-benefits (COB) provision. The COB provisions in group health insurance plans are usually based on the rules developed by the National Association of Insurance Commissioners (NAIC).

   c. Terminated employees (whether voluntary or involuntary) and their covered dependents can retain their group health insurance for a limited period by electing to remain in an employer's plan under the Consolidated Omnibus Budget Reconciliation Act of 1985 (COBRA), which applies to employers of twenty or more employees.

   - The period of extension under COBRA can be up to eighteen months, beginning after a qualifying event that results in the loss of health insurance.

   - Qualifying events can include termination of employment for any reason (except gross misconduct), death of the employee, divorce or legal separation, and attainment of a maximum age by dependent children.

   - If the worker dies, is divorced or legally separated, or has a child who is no longer eligible for coverage, insured dependents can elect to remain in the group plan for up to thirty-six months.

- Workers who elect to remain in the group health insurance plan may have to pay up to 102 percent of the group premium.

6. Both individual and group health insurance plans can include basic medical expense coverages:

   a. Hospital expense insurance

   The benefits provided include those for daily room and board and miscellaneous services and supplies provided during a hospital stay.

   b. Surgical expense insurance

   These are the benefits provided for all expenses related to surgery, including surgeons' fees.

   c. Physicians' visits insurance

   This usually applies when the patient is in the hospital, but sometimes for office visits.

   d. Additional benefits

   These pay for such services as outpatient surgery, preadmission testing, diagnostic x-ray and laboratory expenses, home healthcare services, extended-care facility services, and hospice care.

7. The purpose of major medical insurance is to prevent the insured from being financially ruined by a catastrophic illness or injury. Most insureds are covered under group plans that fall into two categories:

   a. Supplemental plans

   These cover medical expenses that exceed the limits of the underlying basic medical expense policy.

   b. Comprehensive plans

   These combine basic medical expense coverages and major medical insurance into one policy, and are widely used by employers who want both basic and major medical benefits in a single group plan.

C. Government-Provided Health Insurance Plans

   Certain groups receive health insurance under state and federal government programs, including these important health-insurance government-provided or -mandated programs:

   1. Medicare

      a. Medicare is part of the federal Social Security, or Old Age and Survivors Disability Health Insurance (OASDHI) program.

      b. It covers medical expenses of most individuals age sixty-five and older.

  c. Benefits can be paid to disabled individuals under age sixty-five who have been entitled to Social Security disability benefits for twenty-four months (which need not be continuous).

  d. The program also covers persons under age sixty-five who need long-term kidney dialysis treatment or kidney transplants.

  e. The original Medicare program consists of two parts—Hospital Insurance (Part A) and Supplementary Medical Insurance (Part B).

- Medicare Part A is financed largely by payroll taxes, which are paid by both the employee and employer.

- Medicare Part B is financed largely by a monthly premium paid by insured persons and by the federal government's general revenues. Part B covers medical services only when they are medically necessary.

- Individuals can select Medigap policies, from private insurers, that cover the "gaps" that Medicare Parts A and B don't pay, such as deductibles and co-payments.

  f. An alternative Medicare + Choice program (also called Part C) became available in 1997, which enabled beneficiaries to enroll in private health maintenance organizations (HMOs) as well as authorized PPOs.

- The Medicare Modernization Act of 2003 expanded Medicare coverage generally, as well as the original Medicare + Choice plans, which then became known as Medicare Advantage (MA) plans, as the role of private insurers competing to supply coverage for Medicare Part C recipients increased.

- Beneficiaries can choose coverage under a managed care plan, which is a Medicare-approved network of physicians, hospitals, and other healthcare providers that provide care for a fixed monthly fee.

  g. In 2006, Medicare Part D added a prescription drug coverage option for all Medicare beneficiaries to subsidize the cost. Beneficiaries can obtain the Medicare drug benefit through two types of private plans:

- A prescription drug plan (PDP) for drug coverage only

- A Medicare Advantage plan (MA) that covers both medical services and prescription drugs

2. Medicaid

  a. States vary regarding persons covered and types of medical services offered.

  b. Certain medical services are provided in all states, including inpatient and outpatient hospital services, physicians' services, prenatal care, laboratory and x-ray services, and long-term care in nursing homes.

  c. To qualify for benefits, Medicaid applicants must satisfy a stringent means test to show that their income and financial assets (means) are below certain limits.

3. Workers compensation

  a. State workers compensation plans are not strictly health insurance plans or government plans, but they do provide health benefits, as well as disability benefits, and are mandated and regulated by state laws.

  b. Workers compensation plans are not usually provided directly by state governments but instead by commercial insurers.

  c. All states have workers compensation laws that require covered employers to pay benefits to workers who have job-related injuries or diseases.

  d. Workers compensation is based on the liability-without-fault principle, meaning that employers are liable, regardless of fault, for their employees' job-related injuries or diseases.

  e. Most employers must purchase insurance for workers compensation.

4. Other government-provided health insurance plans

  Other health insurance plans are either government provided and/or supported at the federal level, by states, or by both.

  a. For example, the Veterans Health Administration (VA) is funded by the federal government and provides health services and clinical, hospital, and nursing-home care to all eligible veterans.

  b. Some states have other health insurance programs for low-income individuals and families that are either solely state funded and administered or funded jointly with the federal government and administered at the state level.

  c. The State Children's Health Insurance Program (SCHIP), also called the Children's Health Insurance Program (CHIP), is administered by the federal government, which provides matching funds to states for health insurance to families with children.

  d. The Indian Health Service, a federal health insurance program administered by the Department of Health and Human Services, provides public health services to the nearly two million American Indians and Alaska natives who belong to a federally recognized Native American tribe.

Educational Objective 4

Describe the characteristics of the following programs for providing healthcare benefits:

- **Traditional health insurance plans**

- **Managed-care plans**

- **Consumer-directed health plans**

Key Points:

Group and individual (nongroup) healthcare plans in the private, nongovernmental market fall into three categories:

A. Traditional Health Insurance Plans

  1. Traditional health plan providers

   a. Healthcare consumers purchase individual plans from private insurers. Individual consumers include workers with no employer-sponsored health insurance coverage and businessowners with no group coverage.

   b. Life and health insurers, and some property-casualty insurers, offer commercial (private) health insurance (any nongovernmental health coverage) to the public.

   c. Blue Cross and Blue Shield plans historically were not-for-profit plans, although they now are often administered by for-profit organizations.

   - They usually are not described as "commercial insurers" and typically are regulated by state laws separate from those regulating other insurers.

   - These plans cover hospital and physician fees and other medical expenses and offer major medical insurance on either an individual or a group basis.

   - Blue Cross and Blue Shield plans also sponsor managed-care plans.

   - Blue Cross plans usually contract with hospitals and pay them directly rather than paying subscribers (insureds) and Blue Shield plans traditionally have paid physicians directly.

  2. Traditional health insurance plan benefits

   The benefits of traditional health insurance plans from all providers fall into two categories:

    a. Basic medical insurance

    Basic medical expense coverage pays for routine healthcare expenses, for example:

- Hospital expenses
- Surgical expenses
- Physicians' visits
- Additional medical services, such as ambulance and mental health services

    b. Major medical insurance

    Major medical insurance plans provide broader coverage for medical expenses, as well as catastrophic coverage. They typically cover these costs:

- Hospital room and board
- Hospital services and supplies
- X-rays
- Diagnostic tests
- Physician and surgeon services
- Prescription drugs
- Home healthcare services
- Durable medical equipment
- Additional services, such as convalescent nursing-home care and dental services

B. Managed-Care Plans

Managed-care plans not only manage their members' care but also control healthcare costs by contracting with a network of service providers for set fees, compared with traditional plans, in which policyholders select their providers.

    1. Health maintenance organizations (HMOs)

        a. HMOs contract with healthcare providers who agree to provide their services to HMO members at agreed-upon fees.

        b. They exercise certain cost-control procedures:

- Physicians may have to get HMO preapproval for some kinds of treatment.
- HMO members who need a specialist's services must obtain preapproval from a "gatekeeper physician," or primary care physician, thereby preventing unnecessary visits to specialists and ensuring that patients see the appropriate specialists.
- HMOs also determine whether physicians are prescribing excessive or unnecessary diagnostic tests and procedures.

    c. HMOs cover hospital care, physicians' and surgeons' services, laboratory and x-ray services, and outpatient and maternity care, among other services. HMOs pay for these services in full, with few maximum limits, and members pay small co-payments for physician office visits.

    d. HMOs contract with healthcare providers, and members must use those "network" providers. They usually cover only emergency services outside the HMO's geographic area.

2. Preferred provider organizations (PPOs)

    a. A PPO contracts with providers to offer healthcare at a lower cost through either reduced or no co-payments.

    b. Members do not have to use the preferred provider list but generally have lower deductibles and expenses when they do.

    c. PPOs do not require members to maintain a primary care physician or require a primary care physician as a gatekeeper for members to obtain referrals to specialists.

    d. PPOs are one of the more expensive forms of managed-care plans but are also one of the fastest growing because they blend the advantages of both traditional indemnity plans and HMOs.

3. Exclusive provider organizations (EPOs)

    a. An EPO is a network of healthcare providers who have contracted with an insurer to provide healthcare to plan members.

    b. EPO members can use healthcare providers only within an EPO's network, except in emergency situations.

    c. An EPO's insurer reimburses an insured member only when the member receives healthcare services from the provider network.

    d. The network provides services at much lower rates than it would charge otherwise. In turn, the providers receive a guaranteed level of business.

    e. The lower rates charged for healthcare services translate into lower monthly premiums for EPO members.

4. Point-of-service plans (POSs)

    a. A POS plan is similar to both HMOs and PPOs but is more like an HMO.

    b. A POS plan controls medical costs in exchange for more-limited choice.

    c. A member must choose a primary care physician from within a healthcare network, and that primary care physician becomes the member's "point of service."

    d. The primary care physician can refer a member outside the POS network, subject to reduced POS payment for services, which often costs a member significantly more in out-of-pocket expenses.

  5. Medicare Advantage (MA) plans

    a. In addition to the federal government's traditional Medicare program, eligible beneficiaries can receive managed-care services through private insurance plans.

    b. To be eligible to enroll in Medicare Advantage (MA) plans, an individual must be entitled to benefits under Part A and enrolled under Part B of the Medicare program.

    c. These private managed-care choices are part of Medicare Part C.

    d. MA plans offer several managed-care options:
- Health maintenance organizations
- Provider-sponsored organizations
- Preferred provider organizations
- Medical savings accounts (MSAs)
- Private fee-for-service plans (PFFSs)
- Special needs plans (SNPs)

    e. An MA plan must cover all services that are covered by Medicare Parts A and B, plus additional benefits beyond those offered by Medicare.
- These additional benefits may be either a reduction in the premiums, deductibles, and coinsurance payments ordinarily required; healthcare services not covered by traditional Medicare; or both.
- Many MA plans also include Part D prescription drug coverage.

C. Consumer-Directed Health Plans

  1. Consumer-directed health plans (CDHPs) attempt to solve the problem of rising healthcare costs by raising consumer awareness of those costs and giving them more control over healthcare spending.

  2. CDHPs provide consumers with access to high-quality care without subjecting them to deductibles for preventive care.

  3. CDHPs usually include three major components:

    a. A health fund, such as a health savings account (HSA) or a health reimbursement arrangement (HRA)

    b. High-deductible medical coverage, including preventive care not charged against the deductible

    c. Access to informational tools for making informed healthcare decisions

4. Persons covered by CDHPs pay lower premiums for their health coverage because the deductibles are high. Using either an HSA or HRA, they set aside money that can be used to help satisfy the deductible.

   a. HSAs are funded by enrollees themselves, and the money in the HSA can be rolled over for future use at year's end. No taxes are withheld.

   b. The money in an HRA is contributed by the employer and does not count as income. Unused funds in HRA accounts can be rolled over from year to year for future use.

Educational Objective 5

Describe each of the following government programs for providing healthcare benefits:

- **Original Medicare**

- **Medicare Advantage**

- **Medicare Part D Prescription Drug Coverage**

- **Medicaid**

Key Points:

Nearly one-quarter of Americans receive healthcare coverage from Medicare, Medicaid, or both programs. These programs, one federal (Medicare) and one both state and federal (Medicaid), are large and essential parts of the overall American healthcare picture.

A. Original Medicare

1. Medicare, as part of the federal Old Age and Survivors Disability Health Insurance (OASDHI) program, has as its primary goal to provide an affordable healthcare option for the elderly and disabled.

2. Medicare has become the nation's leading healthcare insurance program and covers several groups:

   a. People age sixty-five or older

   b. People under age sixty-five with certain disabilities

   c. People of all ages with end-stage renal disease (permanent kidney failure requiring dialysis or a transplant)

3. The original Medicare program consists of two parts:

   a. Part A (hospital insurance)—Most people do not have to pay for Part A.

   b. Part B (supplementary medical insurance)—Most people pay for Part B on a monthly basis.

4. Payroll taxes paid by both employees and employers largely finance Medicare Part A.

5. Medicare Part B is largely financed through a monthly premium provided by beneficiaries and the federal government's general revenues. The premium is adjusted each year based on plan experience.

6. Medicare Part A helps pay for in-hospital services:

   a. Inpatient care in hospitals

    b. Critical access hospitals (small facilities giving limited out-patient and inpatient services to beneficiaries in rural areas)

    c. Skilled nursing facilities (not custodial or long-term care)

    d. Hospice care

    e. Some home healthcare

7. Most people receive Part A coverage automatically when they turn age sixty-five. Beneficiaries are not required to pay a monthly premium if they or their spouse paid Medicare taxes.

8. Individuals who do not receive premium-free Part A may be able to purchase it under certain conditions:

    a. They are age sixty-five or older, but they (or their spouses) are not entitled to Social Security because they did not work or did not pay enough Medicare taxes while working.

    b. They are disabled but no longer get premium-free Part A because they returned to work.

9. Medicare Part B pays for medically necessary non-hospital services:

    a. Doctors' services

    b. Outpatient hospital care

    c. Some other medical services that Part A does not cover, such as physical and occupational therapy, and some home healthcare

10. Enrolling in Part B is optional. A beneficiary can enroll in Part B any time during a seven-month period that begins three months before turning sixty-five.

11. The premium is usually taken out of monthly Social Security, Railroad Retirement, or Civil Service Retirement payments. Beneficiaries who receive none of those payments must pay the Part B premium every three months.

12. States may help those who have limited income and resources pay for Part A and Part B.

13. Eligibility guidelines are simple, and applicants can get Part A at age sixty-five without having to pay premiums if they meet one or more conditions:

    a. They already receive Social Security or the Railroad Retirement Board retirement benefits.

    b. They are eligible to receive Social Security or Railroad benefits even though they have not yet applied for them.

    c. They or their spouses had Medicare-covered government employment.

14. People who are under sixty-five years of age can get Part A without having to pay premiums if they meet one or more conditions:

 a. They received Social Security or Railroad Retirement Board disability benefits for 24 months.

 b. They have end-stage renal disease and meet certain requirements.

15. Beneficiaries must pay for Part B if they choose to participate in it.

B. Medicare Advantage

 1. Beneficiaries who need more services than Medicare covers can choose private health insurance plans called Medicare Advantage or Part C plans.

 2. The plans, services, and fees of Medicare Advantage vary by location.

 3. Almost all Medicare beneficiaries have access to at least two Medicare Advantage plans, and most have access to three or more.

 a. A private health insurer can deny enrollment based on preexisting conditions.

 b. Medicare pays the Medicare Advantage private health plan a set monthly amount for each beneficiary who participates.

 4. The private plans must offer benefits that at least equal Medicare benefits and must cover everything Medicare covers, but they do not have to cover every benefit in the same way.

 5. A Medicare beneficiary can choose between two types of Medicare Advantage plans:

 a. Managed-care plans

    Also called a coordinated care or Medicare-managed care plan, this can be a basic health maintenance organization (HMO) in which the beneficiary pays a fixed fee and co-payments for various services, subject to conditions:

    • Doctors and hospitals are preferred providers from whom the beneficiary receives services.

    • The beneficiary selects a primary care doctor who refers the beneficiary to specialists when necessary.

    • The beneficiary pays more for services outside the plan.

 b. Private-fee-for-service plans (PFFS)

    • This option allows Medicare recipients to go to any Medicare-approved provider that accepts the plan's payment.

    • The insurer, rather than Medicare, decides how much it and the beneficiary will pay for services.

- The amount paid may be more or less for the benefits Medicare covers and may provide extra benefits Medicare does not.
- The beneficiary must pay the difference to the provider, although Medicare has strict limits on what patients can be charged. The practice of exceeding these limits is referred to as "balance billing."

C. Medicare Part D Prescription Drug Coverage

This is a voluntary program through which the government subsidizes the costs of beneficiaries' prescription drugs underwritten through private insurance carriers and provides coverage for beneficiaries who have very high drug costs or unexpected prescription drug bills.

1. Beneficiaries may sign up for Part D upon first becoming eligible for Medicare (three months before the month they reach sixty-five years of age until three months after they turn sixty-five).

2. If beneficiaries receive Medicare coverage as a result of a disability, they can sign up from three months before to three months after their twenty-fifth month of receiving cash disability payments.

3. Beneficiaries can obtain the Medicare drug benefit through two types of private plans:

    a. A prescription drug plan (PDP) for drug coverage only

    b. A Medicare Advantage plan that covers both medical services and prescription drugs

4. Medicare beneficiaries generally pay monthly premiums for Part D, which vary by plan, and a yearly deductible.

5. Beneficiaries also pay a part of the prescription costs, including a deductible (co-payment) or coinsurance.

6. Those with limited income and resources may qualify for extra governmental assistance and may not have to pay a premium or deductible.

D. Medicaid

Medicaid, a federal-state government healthcare plan, is a means-tested public assistance (welfare) plan for low-income persons, including people with certain disabilities and low-income Medicare beneficiaries requiring nursing home coverage.

1. An investigative process determines whether an applicant is eligible for the program.

2. The federal government pays almost 60 percent of all Medicaid expenses, so while each state administers its own program, the federal Centers for Medicare and Medicaid Services (CMS) set requirements for quality, funding, and eligibility.

   a. Each state must conform to federal guidelines to receive matching funds and grants.

   b. Depending on each state's poverty level, the federal matching formula differs.

   c. Medicaid's costs average 22 percent of each state's budget.

3. Medicaid sends benefit payments directly to healthcare providers. In some states Medicaid beneficiaries must pay a small fee (co-payment) for medical services.

4. Although benefits can vary by state, Medicaid generally covers certain items:

   a. Inpatient and outpatient hospital services

   b. Physician services

   c. Medical and surgical dental services

   d. Some in-home care

   e. Custodial nursing home care

   f. Personal care

   g. Some prescriptions

5. Medicaid provides health insurance coverage to certain categories of low-income individuals:

   a. Children

   b. Pregnant women

   c. Parents of eligible children

   d. People with disabilities

   e. Eligible individuals who have little or no medical insurance

6. Applicants for Medicaid benefits must meet certain requirements:

   a. Age

   b. Pregnancy

   c. Disability

   d. Blindness

   e. Income and resources

   f. Status as a U.S. citizen or a lawfully admitted immigrant

7. Special rules apply to applicants who are disabled children living at home, are living with HIV/AIDS, or are residents of a nursing home.

   a. Disabled children may be covered under Medicaid if they are U.S. citizens or permanent residents. They may be eligible even if their parents are not, or if they live with people other than their parents.

   b. Applicants usually must progress from an HIV-positive diagnosis to AIDS before qualifying under the "disabled" category. More than half of Americans who have AIDS receive Medicaid payments.

8. Once a recipient dies, Medicaid may recover costs paid for healthcare from the recipient's property.

9. Retirees and other individuals facing high nursing home costs are subject to special Medicaid eligibility standards that attempt to prevent them from disposing of substantial assets before applying for Medicaid.

Educational Objective 6

Describe the considerations an individual should review when choosing a long-term care insurance policy, including typical benefits provided or excluded, coverage triggers, eligibility provisions, and other economic issues.

Key Points:

When choosing a long-term care (LTC) policy, a consumer should bear in mind many considerations regarding benefits, coverage triggers, eligibility, and other economic issues.

A. Coverage Basics

   1. Long-term care (LTC) insurance can provide for the daily custodial care as well as the long-term nursing care that an individual may need outside of a hospital.

      a. Neither Medicare nor private medical expense insurance covers long-term care for expenses associated with confinements in such facilities as nursing homes or custodial care centers for extended periods.

      b. Most elderly patients in nursing homes do not initially qualify for long-term care under the strict eligibility requirements of Medicaid, a joint federal and state public assistance program that pays for healthcare for low-income individuals and families.

        • An applicant for Medicaid may have to dispose of assets to qualify for benefits.

        • Some nursing homes do not accept Medicaid recipients.

   2. LTC insurance provides a means to preserve the assets of individuals who require long-term care, as well as the assets of their families.

   3. Individuals can purchase LTC insurance, and some employers offer group plans that enable individuals to obtain coverage at reduced rates.

   4. No standard LTC policy exists, and a consumer should consider several basic aspects of policies when comparing them:

      a. Benefit period
   This is the length of time after filing a claim that the insurer will pay for care (from one year up to lifetime coverage).

     b. Daily benefit

       This is the maximum dollar or percentage amount the insurer will pay for care daily (from about $30 to $300 per day).

     c. Elimination period or deductible

       This is the length of time and the amount of money an insured must pay out of pocket before the insurer starts to pay (from "first day coverage" to a one-year wait).

     d. Level of inflation protection

       This is the amount by which benefits will increase over time to keep up with inflation.

  5. The consumer can choose any combination of benefits, deductibles, or inflation protection options, all of which affect premium cost.

B. Coverage Triggers

  1. A critical LTC policy provision involves the conditions that determine who is eligible to receive benefits, often referred to as coverage triggers.

  2. The most common triggers are activities of daily living (ADLs), medical necessity, and cognitive impairment, which necessitates care to protect the patient and others from threats to safety caused by the patient's condition.

     a. Under most LTC policies, an insured qualifies for benefits when unable to perform a specified number (such as two or three) of the ADLs listed in the LTC policy.

     b. If an insured under an LTC policy with a cognitive impairment trigger is cognitively impaired, the insured qualifies for coverage.

     c. If an insured under the LTC policy meets the medical necessity trigger, coverage for the insured's LTC needs will be provided, subject to the policy limits and provisions.

C. Benefits Typically Provided

  1. Purchasers of LTC insurance typically have a choice of benefits—such as a daily benefit of up to $80, $120, or $160—that is paid over a maximum period of two, three, or four years, or for the insured's lifetime.

  2. Some insurance allows purchasers to select a maximum lifetime benefit amount, such as $300,000.

  3. Some policies provide a maximum benefit equal to the daily dollar limit times the policy duration, subject to a daily maximum dollar limit.

4. A "bed reservation benefit guarantee" holds a bed for a short hospital stay, paying for a number of days to hold a nursing-home bed in case the insured requires hospitalization.

5. The policies typically cover skilled nursing home care, intermediate nursing care, and custodial care.

   a. Many policies also cover home healthcare services.

   b. Few policies cover the cost of having someone come into the home to cook meals, clean the home, or run errands.

6. The majority of LTC policies sold today are comprehensive policies. They typically cover care and services in a variety of long-term care settings, for which they pay daily benefits:

   a. The insured's home, with benefits including skilled nursing care; occupational, speech, physical, and rehabilitation therapy; and help with personal care, such as bathing and dressing

   b. Adult day healthcare centers

   c. Hospice care

   d. Respite care

   e. Assisted living facilities (also called residential care facilities or alternate care facilities)

   f. Alzheimer's special care facilities

   g. Nursing homes

7. Many policies may also pay for services or devices to support insureds living at home:

   a. Equipment such as in-home electronic monitoring systems

   b. Home modification, such as grab bars and ramps

   c. Transportation to medical appointments

   d. Training for a friend or relative to learn to provide personal care safely and appropriately

8. Some policies provide some payment for family members or friends to help care for an insured, but they may do so on a limited basis.

9. Many policies provide the services of a care coordinator, usually a nurse or social worker in the insured's community.

D. Benefits Typically Excluded

   1. The outline of coverage that the consumer receives before applying for coverage and the policy itself list an LTC policy's exclusions, which often follow state regulations regarding what exclusions are allowed.

2. LTC policies have these typical exclusions:
   a. Care or services provided by a family member, unless the family member is a regular employee of an organization that is providing the treatment, service, or care and the organization he or she works for receives the payment for the treatment, service, or care; and the family member receives no compensation other than the normal compensation for employees in the applicable category.
   b. Care or services for which no charge is made in the absence of insurance.
   c. Care or services provided outside the United States, its territories, or possessions. However, a growing number of policies now have an international care benefit that can provide care outside the U.S.
   d. Care or services resulting from a war or an act of war, whether declared or not.
   e. Care or services resulting from an attempt at suicide (while sane or insane) or an intentionally self-inflicted injury.
   f. Care or services for alcoholism or drug addiction (except for an addiction to a prescription medication when administered upon the advice of a physician).
   g. Treatment provided in a government facility (unless otherwise required by law).
   h. Services for which benefits are available under Medicare or another governmental program (except Medicaid); any state or federal workers compensation, employers liability, or occupational disease law; or any motor vehicle no-fault law.
3. Although most policies do not pay for care the insured receives from a family member, friend, or other individual who is not normally paid to provide care, some policies provide a cash payment for each day that the insured receives care from anyone, even if it is a family member or friend.
4. Most policies require that the facility, agency, or individual providing care meet certain minimum standards with respect to quality, safety, and training.
5. LTC policies do not pay for care or services unrelated to meeting the needs of insureds who cannot perform their ADLs on their own or who have cognitive impairment needs.
6. LTC policies do not pay for items provided solely for the insured's comfort or convenience.

E. Inflation Protection
   1. Inflation can substantially erode the real value of LTC insurance benefits.

2. Insurers use two major methods for providing protection against inflation:

    a. Some policies allow insureds to purchase additional amounts of insurance in the future with no evidence of insurability. The premium is based on the insured's current age.

    b. Other policies provide for an automatic benefit increase in which the daily benefit is increased by a specified percentage for a number of years. Adding an automatic benefit increase to a long-term policy is expensive and may double the annual premium in some cases, especially if an insured at an advanced age purchases the policy.

F. Guaranteed Renewability

    1. Most individual LTC insurance policies have guaranteed renewability provisions.

    2. An LTC insurer cannot cancel the policy on the basis of change in the insured's health.

    3. Premiums can be increased for the underwriting class in which the insured is placed.

G. Nonforfeiture Options

    1. Some LTC policies now provide nonforfeiture options.

    2. When the insured cancels an LTC policy, the premiums paid for the policy until the policy is canceled can be returned to the insured or used to purchase the same benefit for a shorter benefit period or a reduced benefit for the existing benefit period while eliminating the need for more premiums.

H. Tax Treatment

    1. An insured who pays more than 7.5 percent of adjusted gross income for medical expenses (including LTC insurance premiums) can deduct those expenses from federal income taxes.

    2. Some special LTC insurance policies are tax-qualified (non-taxed) policies, which makes the LTC benefits tax-free.

    3. Some states allow LTC premium deductions on state income tax returns, regardless of whether a policy is federally qualified.

    4. Employees in group plans generally can pay premiums with pretax dollars, further lowering their costs.

I. Waiver of Premium

    1. This allows, for example, an incapacitated insured to stop paying premiums while receiving benefits and keeping the policy in force with full coverage.

2. In many cases, the premiums must be paid until a time period (usually several months) has been satisfied, and then they are waived.

J. Elimination Period
   1. Most LTC insurance plans are sold subject to an elimination period that functions like a time deductible.
   2. The LTC policy elimination period or deductible is the length of time and the amount of money an insured must pay out of pocket before the insurer starts to pay.
   3. A longer elimination period can substantially reduce the annual premium.

K. Eligibility Provisions
   1. Individual LTC insurance is medically underwritten, meaning that an insurer can refuse an application for a policy from an applicant who does not meet medical guidelines.
   2. Applicants for group policies usually face less-stringent underwriting guidelines than applicants for individual policies.
   3. Age is the primary factor in determining the cost of an LTC policy.
      a. The best time for a consumer to purchase an LTC policy is between ages fifty and fifty-five.
      b. Buying LTC insurance might be desirable before age fifty if the insured has an employer-sponsored group plan.
   4. LTC insurers have varied underwriting guidelines, and many medical conditions are not insurable under most LTC plans. In general, many conditions controlled with medications are insurable.
   5. An applicant who is refused coverage by one insurer might be successful in applying for LTC insurance from another insurer; for example, some LTC insurers specialize in obtaining coverage for high-risk applicants.
   6. All LTC insurance policies have physician certification (or gatekeeper) provisions that determine whether the insured is eligible for policy benefits.

Key Words and Phrases:

Key Words

Preferred provider organization (PPO)
An administrative organization that meets the common needs of healthcare providers and clients and that identifies networks of providers and contracts for their medical services at discounted rates.

Self-insurance plan
An arrangement in which an organization pays for its losses with its own resources rather than by purchasing insurance.

Third-party administrator (TPA)
An organization that provides administrative services associated with risk financing and insurance.

Coordination-of-benefits (COB) provision
Provision that indicates the order of payment when an insured is covered under two or more group health insurance plans so that the insured's total recovery under all applicable policies will not exceed 100 percent of covered expenses.

Indemnity plan
A type of healthcare plan that allows patients to choose their own healthcare provider and reimburses the patient or provider at a certain percentage (usually after a deductible is paid) for services provided.

Major medical insurance
Insurance that covers medical expenses resulting from illness or injury that are not covered by a basic medical expense plan.

Basic medical expense coverage
Coverage for medical expenses, such as hospital and surgical expenses, physicians' visits, and miscellaneous medical services.

Managed care plan
A type of healthcare plan providing members with comprehensive services and incentives to use providers belonging to the plan.

Exclusive provider organization (EPO)
Managed care plan that pays only for medical care received within the network of preferred providers.

Point-of-service (POS) plan
Managed care plan that combines the characteristics of an HMO and a PPO; has a network of preferred providers who, if used by the member, charge little or nothing for services; heathcare received out of the network is covered, but members must pay substantially higher coinsurance charges and a deductible.

Medicare Advantage plans
Health insurance plan options that provide benefits in addition to basic Medicare; offered by private insurers that contract with Medicare and available to beneficiaries currently enrolled in Medicare Part A and Part B.

Private fee-for-service plan
A type of Medicare Advantage plan in which a beneficiary may go to any Medicare-approved doctor or hospital that accepts the plan's payment.

Special needs plan
A special plan providing more-focused healthcare for specific groups of people, such as those who have both Medicare and Medicaid, who reside in a nursing home, or who have certain chronic medical conditions.

Consumer-directed_health_plan
A healthcare benefit plan that combines high-deductible health coverage with a health savings account or health reimbursement arrangement , with resultant lower premiums.

Health savings account
A medical savings account available to consumers enrolled in a high-deductible health plan; the funds contributed to the account are not subject to federal income tax at the time of deposit.

Health reimbursement arrangement (HRA)
An employer-funded medical savings account that reimburses employees for medical expenses not covered by the employer's group insurance plan; distributions to the employee are tax deductible to the employer, and employee reimbursements from the employer are considered tax free.

Medicare
Social insurance program that covers the medical expenses of most individuals age sixty-five and older.

Coinsurance
Medical insurance provision that requires the insured to pay part of the covered medical expenses in excess of the deductible.

Medicaid
Federal-state welfare program that covers the medical expenses of lowincome persons, including those who are aged, blind, or disabled; members of families with dependent children; and pregnant women as well as certain children.

Elimination period
Initial time period in a health insurance or disability income policy during which benefits are not paid.

Time to Take the Next Step....

Congratulations! You have finished the assignments for this course.

If you haven't registered for your exam, you should do so right away while your new knowledge is fresh in your mind.

As another "next step," most students take the SMART Online Practice Exams found on our Web site. The SMART Online Practice Exam not only gives you practice questions, but also helps you learn to manage your time during an exam.

Good luck on your exam! And congratulations on your decision to invest in yourself and your career.